Tea & Antipathy

An American Family in Swinging London

ANITA MILLER

ACADEMY CHICAGO PUBLISHERS

For Mark, Bruce, and Eric. And Jordan.

Copyright © 2015 by Anita Miller
All rights reserved
Published by Academy Chicago Publishers
An imprint of Chicago Review Press, Incorporated
814 North Franklin Street
Chicago, Illinois 60610

ISBN 978-0-89733-743-4

Library of Congress Cataloging-in-Publication Data

Miller, Anita, 1926–
 Tea & antipathy : an American family in swinging London / Anita Miller. —First
edition.
     pages cm
 ISBN 978-0-89733-743-4 (cloth)
 1. Miller, Anita, 1926- 2. Miller, Anita, 1926—-Family. 3. Miller, Jordan, 1926- 4.
Americans—England—London—Biography. 5. Knightsbridge (London, England)—
Biography. 6. London (England)—Biography. 7. Knightsbridge (London, England)—
Social life and customs—20th century. 8. London (England)—Social life and
customs—20th century. I. Title. II. Title: Tea and antipathy.
 DA685.K58M45 2015
 942.1085'6092—dc23
 [B]
                                   2014025481

Cover and interior design: Joan Sommers Design
Cover photo (bottom): Arbyreed

Printed in the United States of America
5 4 3 2 1

Anita Miller founded Academy Chicago Publishers, Ltd, with her husband, Jordan Miller, in 1975. She earned her PhD from Northwestern University, and her doctoral dissertation was published by Garland Publishing. Dr. Miller has written, coauthored, or edited more than seventy-five books including *Uncollecting Cheever: The Family of John Cheever vs. Academy Chicago Publishers, Sharon: Israel's Warrior-Politician,* and *The Fair Women: The Story of the Woman's Building at the World's Columbian Exposition, Chicago 1893.* She has been awarded for distinction in editing and publishing by both London Women in Publishing and Chicago Women in Publishing.

CONTENTS

PREFACE

Mark, fifteen; Bruce, ten; and Eric, seven.

Recently, five of us tried to eat lunch at two o'clock in the afternoon at a restaurant in a New York City hotel. All the tables were empty, but the hostess told us to wait. When I sought her out after ten minutes, she explained cheerfully that she was negotiating with the waitresses to see if one of them would be willing to take our order. They were still discussing it, and she did not see any point in seating us until a definite arrangement had been made.

This tiny incident transported me back more than four decades in time: I could have been standing in a London restaurant in 1965, thinking frostily that nothing like this could ever happen in the United States. As the years have dwindled away, I have thought often of that English summer. Now there is the general nostalgia over John Kennedy, over the Beatles.... It is perhaps a good time to tell the story of our summer vacation in Swinging London, when we began to lose our American innocence.

1

Departure

MY HUSBAND AND I had always been Anglophiles. We had always believed that someday we would move to England and live a life of gentle Jamesian fulfillment. In 1963, as a first step toward the implementation of this dream, Jordan opened a London office of his Chicago press clipping service. For two years he commuted across the Atlantic, in an ever-increasing state of emotional—and financial—disrepair.

I remained at home, coping with our three sons and working on a master's degree in English literature. When I finally got the degree in the spring of 1965, Jordan was so overcome by guilt and the awareness that both he and his business venture had come to the end of their respective ropes that, as a special gift to his neglected family, he rented a house in Knightsbridge for us all for three months.

This announcement filled me with terror. "Three months," I whispered. "What am I going to do with the children in London for three months?" Jordan, home on one of his sporadic visits, looked at me with the contempt of the foraging male for the cowardly cave-hugging female. "London is the most sophisticated city in the world," he said. "If you can't find something amusing to do every day, I really feel sorry for you."

I saw at once that he was right, and fell nervously into line. He was going to spend a fortune, or what was left of a fortune, to make us happy, to atone for his long absence, and only an ungrateful shrew would whine at him about it. We still used words like "shrew" then, in the middle sixties.

Jordan came home to get us at the end of May, and at last we sat together on a British Overseas Airways plane, with Mark, fifteen; Bruce, ten; and Eric seven. As we grew nearer and nearer to the Old World, I could feel gross materialistic provincialism dropping away from us. The sun rose in the middle of the night; Eric woke every two hours, crying hysterically and attempting to stagger down the aisle to what I assume he thought was his bedroom. I had to keep seizing him and hauling him back. Finally the breakfast trays arrived and afterward, pale with excitement and lack of sleep, we saw the green land beneath us.

Sitting in the airport bus, carrying disreputable parcels with socks hanging out of them, I saw with pleasure the familiar black London taxis. I remembered our first visit to England two years before, without the children: smiling hotel porters, jovial waiters, helpful shop assistants. I thought of the Tate Gallery, Kensington Palace, the Burlington Arcade, Hatchard's. I thought of Jane Austen, antique shops, cashmere sweaters, Richard the Lion-Hearted, Penguin Books, country lanes and the stately homes of England. In an upsurge of emotion, I squeezed the arm of my eldest son, who shied like a frightened horse.

"Oh, Mark," I cried, "it's going to be fun!"

2

Arrival

SOMETIME WITHIN the next two hours, we arrived at 16 Baldridge Place, which was to be our home for the summer. Baldridge Place was a quaint eighteenth-century street; all the houses were attached and painted white with gaily contrasting doors. Mrs. Stackpole, who owned Number 16, was unable to come at the moment; the friend she had sent in her place met us on the doorstep, gave us the key, and left without a word.

The distinct odor of mold that hit us in the face when we entered passed rapidly away.

"What's that awful smell?" Eric cried.

"The house is simply old, dear," I responded. "Sometimes old houses smell odd at first. Oh, look at this lovely old sampler on the wall!"

"Eighteen-twenty," Jordan said, reading from it. "Imagine that!"

We found ourselves in a red-carpeted entrance hall; the walls were covered with a red-and-white striped paper that continued up a graceful staircase.

"It's perfect," I said. "A perfect English townhouse."

"I knew you'd think so," Jordan said gratefully. "And wait till you meet Mrs. Stackpole. She's charming."

The little sitting room was rather bare. It did contain an interesting antique mahogany desk and small table, but there was a bulky sofa and matching chair nakedly upholstered in a sort of early Pullman car boucle. "My goodness," I said weakly. "That looks comfortable, doesn't it?"

Jordan, exhibiting some consternation, commented that Mrs. Stackpole appeared to have removed the slipcovers.

"English people are very fond of comfortable furniture," I told the children.

"Boy, is that ugly," Mark said.

The dining room contained only some dark stiff chairs, a little sideboard of a type often seen in Midwestern apartment hotels in the 1930s, a small fire screen with a woman's face embroidered on it, and a stained carpet. "The dining table's gone too," Jordan said. "But I know she'll bring everything back. She's a lovely sort of person, really."

"But look at those beautiful velvet curtains," I said.

We all trailed down to the kitchen, in the basement.

"Why is the kitchen in the basement?" Eric asked.

"These houses were designed for servants," I said. "A long time ago." I went on to explain that Americans were spoiled, expecting everything at their fingertips, and it would be very good for us to climb a few stairs for a change.

Some efforts had apparently been made to update the kitchen: pipes were chopped into the walls and ceiling; the floor was covered with a lumpy, red linoleum, inexpertly patched together.

"Wow, look at this stove," Bruce said. "It doesn't light."

The stove, its iron legs gracefully bowed, stood in the old hearth, under a high narrow mantelpiece. Across the oven door was printed in Gothic script: *The New World*. "It must date from Columbus," Mark said.

"We're all too materialistic at home," Jordan said. "Anyone will tell you that."

Bruce made a second attempt to light one of the burners. "None of these stoves are automatic," Jordan remarked, with some impatience. From the warming rail, he picked up a sort of battery with a long curved neck. "You just press this button. You light English gas stoves with these clever little batteries."

"Isn't that clever," I said, after a minute.

"You're lucky to have a nice white sink and a refrigerator," Jordan said to Mark.

"I am?" Mark said.

Next to the kitchen was what appeared to be a playroom with a blue linoleum floor, and down the hall was a laundry room; there was a new-looking washing machine in it. Jordan said that Mrs. Stackpole had told him that the washing machine was broken.

We went back upstairs to the ground floor, and then up the curving staircase to a landing where there were bookshelves in an alcove, and a bathroom with a green linoleum floor: decals of Bo-Peep and Little Mary Quite Contrary were pasted on the tub and the sink.

"Isn't that cute," I said.

We went up some more stairs and found ourselves in the master bedroom: a large airy room with tall windows. It might once have been the drawing room. "Everything's got flowers on it," Mark said.

"That's chintz," I said. "I mean, that's chintz on the chairs and the settee and those throw pillows."

"How come it doesn't match?" Mark asked.

"Oh, match, match," I said. "Why does it have to match? This has a definite charm of its own. There's nothing wrong with mixing a few patterns."

The bead of the king-sized bed was shoved up against the carved mantelpiece that held two lamps with flounced shades and a lot of dangling crystals. Above it hung a dark, rather sticky-looking painting of a fat lady clutching a book with her eyes turned upward, while some other fat ladies looked over her shoulder and some fat angels floated around them.

"Hey, that's cool," Mark said.

We looked at him suspiciously.

"I mean it's cool," he explained. "It's old or something."

"Oh, it's old all right," Jordan said quickly. "I mean I'll bet it's a Renaissance painting or something."

"There's another fat lady over here," Bruce said, pointing above the chest of drawers, from which the veneer was peeling in strips.

"Boy, is that old," Mark said, looking at the chest.

"I don't know why everything has to be perfectly new and neat all the time," I said. I was feeling rather tired. Jordan agreed that that sort of attitude was middle-class.

"When you meet Mrs. Stackpole, Mark, you'll understand. She's certainly not middle-class."

"I can see that," Mark said. He opened a door, revealing an enormous bathroom with pale green plumbing and a wallpaper pattern different from the one in the bedroom. But flowered curtains tied the decor of the two rooms together.

"More flowers," Jordan said, laughing nervously. He pointed proudly to a collection of wires over the bathroom door. "An electric fire. I'll tell you about it some other time. And they call this towel rack a 'hot rail'. It keeps towels dry."

Up another flight of stairs were the children's rooms. One, with a flowered carpet, a yellow quilted spread and pictures of dogs all over the walls, was perfect for Mark.

"This must be the Nanny's room," I whispered, impressed.

"What's that?" Eric asked. "A goat?"

The large nursery had little cots, slippery rugs, and watercolors of Victorian children with long pale ringlets and wistful eyes. A marble sink stood near the window.

"Oh, isn't this charming," I cried. "It's a little musty, though. Let's open the window."

I wanted to get the children to bed. It upset me that Bruce and Eric should have been up nearly all night. I was afraid that at any moment something awful would happen to them: they would faint or become hysterical, develop tuberculosis or a tropical disease like ringworm or blight. So it was with great relief that I saw them into their cots, which were made up with strange strips of blue nylon instead of sheets. The fresh air dispelled somewhat the musty odor of the room. I had noticed, however, that the odor grew stronger as one approached the marble sink and that it carried with it more than a hint of sewer gas. I decided to say nothing about it, however, and so, feeling tired but happy, we went to bed, under the sticky painting of the woman with the turned-up eyes.

3

The Inventory

A FEW HOURS into our nap, the doorbell rang. Jordan went downstairs to greet Mrs. Stackpole, who had arrived to conduct the inventory. After combing my hair and trying in general to make myself presentable, I followed him down to find sitting at the desk, not the middle-aged lady in tweeds with a firm handclasp whom I had envisioned, but a slender creature whose brown bouffant hairdo peeped from under a little kerchief.

"Mrs. Miller," she said, fluttering long lashes and leaning toward me with intense sincerity. "There's such a lot of noise and traffic in the street here. Is that all right?"

I said it was, and we began to go through the inventory of ground floor items: two armchairs, one sofa, two tables.... Jordan interrupted to ask her diffidently what had happened to the dining room table.

"Oh, it's being mended," Mrs. Stackpole said. "A little man will bring it round. You couldn't have used it the way it was."

"And the slipcovers?" Jordan asked.

"Oh, yes," she responded vaguely. "Do you like those?" She looked at her watch. "I'm just off to Ascot," she said, with an apologetic laugh.

We were impressed by that; it sounded suitably upper class. We followed her trim figure in its quiet blue coat down the basement stairs into the kitchen. She began to open cupboards and count things.

"*Six* teacups," she read from her thin inventory sheets and pointed to the teacups that were actually mugs, one odder than the others, bearing a picture of a monkey in a dress holding an umbrella. "*One*, two, three, four," she said, counting. There was an awkward pause. She consulted the paper. "*Six* teacups," she read again. Reassured, she turned back to the shelf. "One, two, three, four...."

We watched her, mesmerized. The paper. "Six teacups." The shelf. "One, two, three, four...." There was an admirable persistency in Mrs. Stackpole's character. After another lingering moment of silent count, she took a pencil from her smooth blue calf bag and made an emendation to the inventory sheet. "*Four* teacups," she said, smiling at us with all her dimples. We smiled back.

Pointing to the mantel over what we will laughingly call the stove, she said: "Two pots." Pointing under the wood-enclosed white porcelain sink: "Two casseroles." She met my eyes with her blue level gaze. "I'm sorry," she said. "I could only get these two small casseroles."

"Oh, it's all right," I said quickly. "I can use two for one casserole."

"Two for one casserole," she murmured, pleased. "Of course."

We had apparently completed the list of cooking utensils. I had a dim idea that something was missing, but I couldn't think what it could be. I asked myself, *Do I do all my cooking in two pots and two small casseroles?* I couldn't remember.

"Mr. Miller asked me to leave my good dishes," Mrs. Stackpole went on, whipping open a sliding panel that promptly fell off. "So I have. They can quite easily be replaced if they are broken." She disclosed a set of interesting china: red peacocks paraded around the rims of the dishes, alternating with yellow doodles. "These can all quite easily be replaced," she repeated, with slight emphasis. It developed later, in a moment of need, that the set consisted of twenty or thirty luncheon dishes, ten or twelve dinner dishes, a toast rack and a cream jug.

Mrs. Stackpole then turned her attention to the large kitchen dresser, upon which stood some egg cups and a little clay figure with a basket on its back, possibly for toothpicks. "One duck," Mrs. Stackpole read, enunciating clearly. "I left you some cookery books," she went on, opening a drawer, and then she explained the stove to me. Actually no one could explain the stove to me; its continued existence in the middle of the twentieth century was, and will remain, a mystery. But she tried. "Your kitchen towel," she said, pointing gaily to a blackish object hanging limply on the back of a door; then, to a longer, greasy, more frightful object on a hook: "Your apron!"

After explaining that every Thursday we had to wind the large cream-colored thing in the corner, she walked quickly out of the kitchen and down the passage to the laundry room. "There's your ironing board and iron," she said. There was a moment of silence. "I'm afraid the washing machine doesn't work," she said, smiling.

"Maybe," Jordan said, "we can get it re—"

"Actually," Mrs. Stackpole said, "it does work. I told you it didn't, but it does." She turned to me, her eyes begging for forgiveness. "Would you mind very much not using it? I saved up for it for ever so long, and it's ever so precious, would you mind not...?"

"Of course not," I said, rather stiffly.

"And here's your clothesline," she said, trying to open a door with five or six burglar-proof locks on it.

"We won't need that," I said. "We'll take the clothes to the launderette."

"Oh, there's one ever so near," Mrs. Stackpole cried happily. "It won't be difficult for you at all." She moved rapidly back down the hall to the playroom with the blue linoleum floor. "And here are all my children's playthings," she said, allowing us to see a blackboard, a rocking horse, a little desk, several touching crayon drawings of crooked houses and lopsided ladies, and a cupboard stuffed with teddy bears. "They're all ever so precious to them, so you *will* just keep this door closed, won't you, and not let anyone use it? It's just their precious little bits."

I could feel my smile stiffening again. It's just their precious little bits, I said to myself, keep your shirt on. Later on, when Eric became frightened by Hamlet's uncle and refused to stay upstairs alone, he kept creeping into the playroom and nearly drove us crazy playing "Rudolph the Red-nosed Reindeer" over and over on Mrs. Stackpole's children's precious little phonograph which had a straight pin in it instead of a needle. In addition, he wrote "Ringo" in a wavering hand on the upper left-hand corner of the blackboard and we allowed the desecration to remain.

Before we left the nether regions, Mrs. Stackpole mentioned that she had locked all *her* precious bits and pieces in the "cupboard," which proved to be the kitchen pantry. "So you won't have to be bothered with looking after them," she explained. "But you can quite easily keep all your groceries and things in here," she went on, leading us back down the passage toward the laundry room again, and opening a door beneath the stairs to reveal a damp darkness, in the depths of which we could distinctly hear the scurrying of many startled little feet. "That will work out quite well for you," Mrs. Stackpole said, beaming at me.

We followed her upstairs to the bathroom on the landing to discuss the linen, Mrs. Stackpole remaining ebullient and persistently pleasant as she explained to us why she had left only two sheets for our bed. "If I leave you the other two I own, I won't have any clean ones when I get back."

Neither of us understood this, but we both pretended we did. I kept nodding and smiling.

"I've bought nylon sheets for the children's beds," she told us, aspirating the final syllable of "nylon" in the French way, "and here are your four towels. I'm afraid they're all I have for you."

Still nodding and smiling, we descended to the living room or drawing room or whatever it was.

"By the way," Mrs. Stackpole said, "Miss Pip, the young lady who is renting the top floor in the autumn, has asked permission to bring in a few things one afternoon. Is that all right?"

I nodded, smiling.

"Please tell me if it isn't," Mrs. Stackpole said earnestly, leaning toward me in her solicitous way, "because it can quite easily be put off until you are out of the house."

"Oh, it's perfectly all right," I said. "One afternoon?"

"Oh, just one afternoon," Mrs. Stackpole said. "Is that all right?"

"Certainly," Jordan said.

"You're sure?"

We were sure.

"And I've left six or seven vases in the back lavatory," she said. "It seems a lot, but one never knows, one frequently needs many vases."

"Oh yes," I said. "I do like my vases."

"Here is a list of things—grocers who will deliver, laundries, things of that sort."

She produced more papers.

"Plumbers... And Mrs. Grail will be here tomorrow. She's Irish, and quite honest and dependable. You may give her a key if you like. It's *quite* all right." I could only admire her assurance. I knew that she *must* be correct; she had an instinct for it. It was an instinct that I notably lacked. "I intend to retain her myself when I return in the autumn," Mrs. Stackpole added.

"Will she cook dinner for us?" I asked, thinking of The Stove.

She paused to consider. "She'll have to go home to feed her family. They eat at five or six. I don't see why she couldn't come back to serve *your* dinner at eight."

Since our dinnertime was approximately the same as Mrs. Grail's, I could see that I would have to cope with The Stove myself.

"Now the slipcovers..." Jordan began.

"Oh, yes." She blushed prettily, smiling. "They're being mended. They didn't fit properly."

"Well, would you just jot down the name and number of the shop? In case we need to call them."

"Oh yes, of course." She wrote something quickly on the back of our list, and said, "I've left some eggs in the refrigerator. It's so difficult to leave food when one doesn't know... er... other's... habits...."

Gathering herself together to depart, she paused to leave us some keys: two front door, three back door, and twelve or fifteen odd-looking gold-and-black ones.

"These are keys to the burglar locks," she said to me. "You can't open the windows without them, and you must remember always to lock the windows with these keys when you close them. Please remember *never, never* to leave the doors or the windows unlocked when you go out. I can't emphasize this strongly enough. All the houses around here have been broken into at one time or another. They watch, you see, and they know when you go out. Even if you go out for only a few minutes, you *must* lock all the doors and windows. It's terribly important."

"It would be difficult for them to climb in a bedroom window," I said nervously.

"They're much more apt to come over the roofs, aren't they?" she asked calmly. I looked at the houses across the street: the rooftops were peaked, gabled, with crooked Dickensian chimneypots silhouetted against the gloomy sky. Could someone crouch there, behind a peak or gable, and watch...?

"Please don't lose the keys," Mrs. Stackpole said at the door. "These are the only ones and it costs thirty pounds to replace the lock. And do remember to lock the windows. You can open them when you're *in* the house, of course." She called over her shoulder as she went out, "And remember, if you need anything, there's always Mr. MacAllister, isn't there?"

"Who's that?" I asked Jordan, when the door had closed.

"Some man," he said vaguely. "Her boyfriend, I guess."

"Her fiancé, you mean," I said. "I suppose he sends her the flowers for all those vases."

"I'd better go out and get some bread and butter to go with those eggs," Jordan said. He looked at his watch. "It's five-thirty, but I think there's a delicatessen in South Ken that stays open late." I should explain that in those days London shops closed at five o'clock, except for Early Closing on Wednesday and Saturday at one in the afternoon.

"Maybe you ought to call a plumber before you go," I said. "Something's wrong with the toilet."

"Nothing's wrong with the toilet," he said. "I can tell you that right now. It's an English toilet, that's all. Just pump the handle gently up and down and eventually it will flush."

I found this difficult to believe, because I felt that when the English did something, they *had* to do it at least as well as Americans. But I let it go, and he went off in the rain to find provisions.

I descended into the kitchen to assemble my tools, and suddenly I realized that Mrs. Stackpole had not left me a frying pan. I thought this was very odd, but there must have been some explanation for it. "I'll boil the eggs," I said aloud. This seemed more English to me anyway: boiled eggs for tea. I took down the large pot from the mantel: it had a greenish wet pool in the bottom and several hunks of enamel missing.

"Not to worry," I said, still cheerful. "The eggs have a shell." I noticed with a clutch of anguish that there was no electric toaster. I was appalled at my weakness: toast could of course be made under the stove grill, two pieces at a time. "Americans are terribly spoiled," I said sternly to myself, avoiding the sight of the "hot cloth" hanging, black and dispirited, over the pipe.

Soot was falling down the ancient chimney; it fell behind the stove and blanketed the warming rail. "A real English kitchen," I said. The boiler exploded softly in the comer.

4

Slipcovers

THE NEXT MORNING we were awakened early by a messenger delivering an enormous bouquet from Mrs. Stackpole.

"I told you she was kind," Jordan said.

"Really thoughtful," I murmured, overwhelmed by this huge assortment of lilies and roses and I didn't know what all, not being horticultural. "It's a good thing she left all those vases."

While we were dealing with the bouquet, the bell rang again, this time heralding the entrance of Mrs. Grail, the cleaning woman, a pleasant-looking, plump person with short curly gray hair, decently attired in a black sweater and skirt. "Don't worry about a thing," she said, in a rich brogue. "She's told me where everything is. Ah! The lovely flowers!"

"Yes, aren't they? Mrs. Stackpole sent them."

"Ah, God," Mrs. Grail said. "They must have cost her a pretty penny. And she hasn't that much to spare."

"Yes, it was kind of her."

"It looks like a funeral." Her eye swept the sitting room. "She's cleared it out, hasn't she? And where are the slipcovers?"

I picked up the list from the desk. "They're being mended," I said.

"Mended, is it?" said Mrs. Grail. "They looked new to me."

'They're being mended. She wrote the name of the shop right here." I turned the paper over. In her large clear hand, Mrs. Stackpole had written, "Glenairlie, Pitwee, Firth."

"There must be some mistake," I said. "I think this is her address in Scotland."

"There's no mistake," Mrs. Grail said grimly.

I went upstairs to Jordan, who was shaving in the bathroom.

"Look," I said. "She wrote her Scottish address here instead of the name of the shop with the slipcovers."

"Oh, she's so absent-minded," Jordan said, with a chuckle.

"I don't think Mrs. Grail likes her," I said.

"Ridiculous," he responded. "It's probably just Mrs. Grail's way."

The phone rang, two short bleeps. Eric answered it and handed it to me. It was Mrs. Stackpole.

"Which child was that?" she asked. "I don't know which child that was."

I told her it was Eric, the youngest.

"Ah," Mrs. Stackpole said fondly. "The wee one."

"Well, he's seven. And we do want to thank you for the flowers. They're so beautiful."

"Oh, it was because Mr. Miller seemed to miss so many of my little bits. Pictures of the children, and so on. I'm afraid it looked a bit bare."

"Well, it was kind of you. By the way…"

"Might I have a word with your husband?"

"Oh, yes," I said. "Only I don't know how it happened, but you wrote your—"

"I'm afraid I'm in a bit of a hurry," Mrs. Stackpole said pleasantly. "I would just like a word with your husband."

"Ask her about the slipcovers," I whispered, handing him the phone.

"Yes," he said. "Oh, it was lovely of you. You didn't need to. Yes, I have your address. Yes, I'll drop it in the mail. Yes. By the way—oh, yes. Listen, you forgot to leave the number of the slipcover man. Yes, you remember. His phone number. Oh. Well, what's his name and address then? Yes, but I'd like that in case he doesn't return them. When were they promised? Oh, but that's a month from now. I mean, it's only early June now. Give me his address and I'll try to hurry him."

There was a pause. "Oh," Jordan said. "Well, all right if you… Yes."

He hung up, looking puzzled. "She says he's not on the telephone, he's just a little man. I couldn't exactly get his address. Anyway, she finally said she's got a spare pair, locked away in a cupboard. She'll come and get them out."

"Do you mean they've been here all the time? Why didn't she put them on the furniture?"

"Maybe they're too ratty-looking," Jordan said. "How about that little man who's not on the telephone? I suppose he's too little to reach the receiver?"

He went off to the office, amid waves of merriment. Soon the doorbell rang, and Mrs. Stackpole appeared in the hall, her hair blown, her eyes wild. "I must rush," she cried, leaping up the stairs. In a moment she leaped down again, empty-handed. "I've brought the key to the wrong cupboard," she cried. "I'll be back."

"What a shame," I said to Mrs. Grail. "She'll miss her train."

Mrs. Grail grunted, leaning on her Hoover. "It's too many cupboards and too many keys," she said. "You won't see her again."

"Oh, but she *said*..."

Mrs. Grail turned to her machine. "It's the English, you know," she said enigmatically, and pushed the switch. I hung around for a while, peering out the window through the glass curtain. I was just about to go upstairs and get dressed, when the bell rang again, and Mrs. Stackpole vaulted into the house like an alarmed gazelle. She bounded up the stairs, Mrs. Grail trailing after her, dragging the Hoover. In a few minutes Mrs. Stackpole came panting down, her arms filled with polished chintz slipcovers: large green flowers on a cream-colored background. They looked perfectly presentable to me.

"I'm terribly sorry to have kept you waiting," she said, breathing heavily. "Here they are. The larger one is for the sofa and the smaller one is for the armchair." She paused to let that information sink in. "The very small ones cover the cushions, of course. Mrs. Grail can help you. I must fly. Just tell your husband Mr. MacAllister will call round for the money," she added, and was gone.

I began laboriously to stuff the cushions into the slipcovers. Mrs. Grail came into the sitting room and stood behind me.

"They're very nice for a spare pair, aren't they?" I said.

Mrs. Grail sniffed. "Well, they're the very ones," she said. "They're the very ones was here the day I came to see her. They're the only ones she's got."

"But... Maybe they're identical...."

"Well, I stood there just now when she got them out, you know. I said, 'Aren't those the very slipcovers I saw, Mrs. Stackpole?' And she said, 'Yes, Mrs. Grail. I'm afraid they are.'"

"She lied to us," I said, dumbfounded.

"It's the English, you know," Mrs. Grail told me seriously. "They'll do you every time."

5

Pat Foyle

FEELING RATHER SHAKEN, I went upstairs to get dressed. Our first afternoon in London was already arranged for us. The children and I would meet Jordan for lunch and then I would shop for groceries. The office manager's assistant, a girl named Jane, was coming to take us to the city.

When the bell rang, I tripped down the stairs to meet Jane. I had expected a junior executive type, sort of Debbie Reynolds with a dash of Rosalind Russell: crisply efficient, in a knit suit, small pearl earrings, and white gloves. (This was the mid-sixties, remember.) Instead I found a young person with bangs touching her nose, a great deal of long straight hair obscuring the rest of her face, wearing a cotton two-piece dress several sizes too big for her, baggy green textured stockings and lopsided shoes with run-over heels. Eric immediately fell completely in love with her: what you could see of her face was very pretty. She addressed me in incomprehensible tones, with a faint smile. I nodded and smiled back, although I had no idea what she was saying, and off we went, for our first ride on a red double-decker London bus. We sat on top, and lurched forward for half an hour on what seemed to our transatlantic eyes to be the wrong side of the road, past massive buildings, colored gray.

We clambered down in the middle of the financial district. "I could have had us get off farther up and saved a walk," Jane said. "Sorry about that." We didn't mind a walk; it was all new and exciting. Everybody looked exotic to us. The children kept edging close to newspaper stands looking for Beatle magazines; Jane strode on with never a backward glance. We turned a corner and came to a very large building with a marble entryway. Jordan's offices were on the ground floor. You had to walk past the elevator—a sort of circular cage cut into the center of the floor—and then you came to the offices of Pressclips U.K. Ltd.

The offices seemed a bit grimy; cold light filtered through grayish glass. But there was a great deal of activity: frazzled people with lumpy hair scurried about carrying things. I didn't remember seeing so many people rushing about in Jordan's Chicago premises. At the end of the corridor, behind a door with a frosted glass pane, we found Jordan in the office he shared with Bill Dworkin, a Chicago employee—originally a native of New Jersey—whom Jordan had brought over to run Pressclips U.K. I noted that Bill had grown a beard. He was drinking tea from a blue cup with a broken handle. A very tall Englishman slouched in a straight chair, with his legs thrust out before him. Jordan introduced him as Pat Foyle; he said he had written me about him.

The name was familiar, but the details were lost in a welter of letters about Pats and Teensies and Allans and Basils. It seemed to be easy to make friends in London. Or at least it seemed to be easy for Jordan, who was trusting and gregarious. We strolled off to a restaurant, Jordan in front with the children and me behind with Pat. Bill had stayed in the office, sipping moodily from his blue cup. "Look out for American tourists," he called after us. "They'll jostle you off the curbing."

"What do you think of all this?" Pat asked, gesturing vaguely.

"Oh," I said, "it's very exciting. I've always loved England."

"Jordan will have you living here yet," he said, chuckling.

"Well," I said doubtfully.

There was a long pause. "I can't get used to no screens on the windows," I said finally, having thought of something to say. "I keep expecting mosquitoes."

"Skeeters?" Pat asked. "I think the time is past for skeeters."

"You do have them here then?" I asked, surprised.

"Skeeters? Oh, I expect so."

"What?"

"I'll ask," Pat said.

We went into the upstairs room of a restaurant filled with Victorian atmosphere. It seemed fitting: in spite of the heavy traffic, all the streets had a touch of Victorian ambience. Workmen wore large caps and long aprons; each office had a snub-nosed boy to run errands. To my surprise, I did not find this exhilarating. Despite my romantic predilection for the past, I felt a little strange, a little out of place. And I didn't feel hungry; that was proof that something was wrong.

I sampled Bruce's steak and kidney pie: to my vast disappointment, it tasted like liver. "Bring cokes for these young Americans," Pat said expansively to the waiter. The cokes came with lemon and no ice.

"It's got lemon in it," Eric said loudly. "And it's warm."

"I suppose you want ice," Pat said. He turned to me. "And you want ice water, I suppose."

"I'd like some gin with anything," I said.

"Ice water is what makes Americans effete," Pat said, joking.

"I hate this coke," Eric said.

"Wait until you meet my little girl," Pat said to Bruce and Eric. "You'll love her."

He slouched back in his chair. "She's beautiful," he said. "I haven't seen her for a while, but I'm going to see her Friday, I think."

I drank my gin and thought about Mrs. Stackpole's kitchen. I was thinking I would have to cook something in it and I didn't know what to cook or where to get it, and I didn't remember anything Mrs. Stackpole had said about the stove, which I was trying to forget anyway.

Suddenly lunch was over and Jordan stood up. "Well, I'm going back to the office now," he said.

We looked at him dumbly. It occurred to the four of us simultaneously that we were sitting in a room in the middle of an enormous city full of strangers. It was raining mistily outside and the rest of the afternoon stretched before us.

"I'll stay in the office and help you, Dad," Mark said.

"I want to help too," Bruce said.

"I want to help too," Eric said. "I want to see Jane."

"You can help later," Jordan said. "Mark will help today."

Mark looked relieved.

"What are we going to do?" Bruce asked. It was the very question that had occurred to me.

"Sightsee," Jordan said, avoiding my eyes. "Look around. Go to a museum. The Victoria and Albert is right near the house."

"I'll go off with you," Pat said. "Show you round."

We went off in a taxi toward Knightsbridge. "Take them round Buckingham Palace and all that jazz," Pat said to the driver. He took us round Buckingham Palace and then round Westminster. Pat pointed out the statue of Abraham Lincoln and remarked that Englishmen never assassinated *their* leaders. I accepted this: all my life I had believed in the Englishman's sense of Fair Play, his sturdy honesty, his good nature, his instinctive good taste, his intellectual endowments, his aversion to violence. Pat himself was not only slender and handsome, but friendly, and he had a beautiful accent.

After we had seen all the jazz, he took us to Harrods in the Brompton Road, very near Baldridge Place, and led us through the food halls and the bank. Then he left us, reluctantly, because he had an appointment. We roamed the food halls and then walked outside for a while, but it was raining. There was a Wimpy's across the street. Since I had not nerved myself to buy anything in the food halls, I decided on take-out hamburgers and fries for that night. Only as a stop-gap, I thought sternly, because after all Wimpy's was part of the Americanization of London which God knew all right-thinking people deplored.

When we opened the door to Baldridge Place the telephone was ringing. I approached it with caution. "Hello?" I said.

"Anita!" cried a friendly voice. "This is Cynthia!" Cynthia was a friend of mine from Chicago, an English girl, married to an American, who had returned to London for two months to visit her parents. We had telegraphed her our phone number because her parents did not have a phone.

"Oh, Cynthia," I said, beginning to babble. "Oh my goodness, how are you, Cynthia? My goodness, it's great to hear your voice. Where are you?" She was about an hour away, but she said she and her daughter Sydney, who was Bruce's age, were coming to see us and spend the day. "Cynthia and Sydney are coming here tomorrow," I announced. "And we'll spend the whole day together!"

"Oh, boy," Bruce said. "That's great."

6

Cynthia

THE NEXT DAY was dull and gray. We were enlivened by the prospect of the visit with Cynthia and Sydney, and by the arrival of the man to install the rented television set.

"Oh, I can hardly wait," I said to Jordan, who was putting on his coat in the hall. "English television must be really marvelous."

"Well," Jordan said.

"What do you mean?" I asked, annoyed. "It *must* be great. The BBC and all that. Those actors and everything."

"Yeah, I know," Jordan said. "But I watched it a lot last winter...."

"And?"

"Well, I don't know...."

"You must have been tired," I said firmly. "It has to be great. The BBC and all that. Drama."

"Well," Jordan said. He left under a slight cloud with Mark.

The children and I dressed quickly. I had seen a great deal of Cynthia during the past few years. She couldn't drive and I enjoyed taking her shopping, and to lunch. I knew that she missed England, and I sympathized with her. Besides, in addition to being pretty, she was always friendly, polite and good-natured—qualities which I always felt were at least partly due to her early environment and upbringing.

"In many ways she's my closest friend," I said to Mrs. Grail, who was washing the breakfast dishes.

"I've been meaning to ask you," Mrs. Grail said. "Where are the sheets?"

"Well," I said.

"It'll soon be time to change them," Mrs. Grail said.

"Well," I said, "I'm afraid there aren't any other sheets, Mrs. Grail."

"How do you mean?"

"I mean there aren't any others because Mrs. Stackpole doesn't have any. I mean she has another pair but if she leaves them all, then she won't have any clean ones when she gets back."

"How's that?" Mrs. Grail wiped her hands on her apron and turned to face me.

"I'm not sure," I confessed.

"You mean she only left you the one pair? And them twisty things on the boys' beds?"

"They're nylon," I said faintly. The bell rang at this point. "Oh, there's Cynthia," I said thankfully, and headed for the basement stairs.

"And no frying pan," Mrs. Grail called after me. I went hastily up the stairs and opened the front door to find Cynthia and Sydney on the stoop.

"Oh, Cynthia," I said. "How are you?"

"Well, well," Cynthia said. "So this is the town house."

"Yes, it's charming," I said.

I showed her around the house. She seemed particularly interested in the nursery. "Where's Mary Poppins?" she asked. I noticed a certain ironic edge to her voice that seemed new. I couldn't remember hearing it before. "Aren't you feeling well, Cynthia?" I asked.

"Well, I don't know how I can be expected to feel," Cynthia said. "My mother and father are getting older and I can't be here to take care of them."

I began to prepare cheese sandwiches. "I suppose that is upsetting," I said, getting out the bread.

"Well, I don't know what else you would call it," Cynthia said.

I served the cheese sandwiches and then we all went for a walk through Knightsbridge. "Knightsbridge is very posh, I believe," Cynthia said.

"Yes, it's close to everything. And the shops are nice."

"Oh, it's posh," Cynthia responded. We stopped on the street so that Bruce could buy some peanuts from a vendor. "Oh Sydney," Cynthia said, "I hope *you're* not going to eat those dreadful peanuts."

"What's wrong with peanuts?" I asked.

"Eating peanuts in the street," Cynthia said. She kept looking around nervously.

At this point the children announced that they were thirsty. It was getting on for teatime anyway, so we went into a large tea shop in the Brompton Road.

"I imagine it's quite elegant in here," Cynthia whispered to me. I didn't see why she thought so: the tablecloths were not clean, the walls were a bilious yellow and the chairs had a hard institutional look. We took a table anyway, Cynthia sidling along in a peculiar obsequious manner like a clerk ushering Scrooge into an inner office. We ordered mineral water and teacakes.

There were two people at a table in the front of the shop, about a quarter of a mile away, and the usual hostess with sausage curls wandering about, but Cynthia kept addressing Sydney in a constrained whisper. "Oh, stop eating those peanuts, Sydney. Straighten your collar. Don't slump."

No one seemed to be paying any attention to us. The people at the front table were looking out the window, the hostess had gone into the kitchen, and Sydney and Bruce and Eric went on eating peanuts and drinking warm mineral water.

"Oh, this is disgraceful," Cynthia said hoarsely. "I forbid you to eat those peanuts, Sydney. Oh, how terrible this is."

Cynthia was casting a pall over teatime. Her personality seemed to have undergone a transformation of some sort. Apparently an old feeling of social inferiority had been fanned into violent existence by the Knightsbridge atmosphere. I decided I liked Cynthia better when she was in Skokie.

After tea we went shopping. I paused in Woolworth's to buy a frying pan because that was where Mrs. Grail had told me to get one; then we went into a large supermarket so that Cynthia could help me choose groceries. Still speaking in an unusually low voice, and casting self-conscious glances left and right, Cynthia pointed to shelves and bins and freezers.

"Of course Australian beef is cheaper," she said, "but as you can see it's frozen and Mummy always buys British beef. There's nothing like it, or English lamb either. English tomatoes are certainly the best and we only use Danish butter at home. I think you ought to taste real fish for a change, I doubt if you've ever had it."

I tumbled everything obediently into my cart and was jolted, when I reached the checkout counter, to discover that I was expected, after emptying the cart, to bag my own groceries.

It wasn't what I was used to. I asked the clerk whether they delivered. "Certainly," she said. "In the morning only." I began to bag everything; the clerk checked out others behind me who pushed and shoved and fell against me while they were stuffing their purchases into their bags. Cheeses rolled on the floor as Cynthia and I worked, sweating, and the clerk kept giving us annoyed glances. Finally we staggered out, loaded with sacks and the frying pan, and walked Cynthia and Sydney to the bus stop.

"I'm inclined to follow you around all day, holding your skirt and sucking my thumb," I said, making a joke out of it.

Cynthia smiled coldly. "I'm terribly depressed, you know," she said. "I really don't have time to think about much because my parents are getting older and I can't stay here to take care of them."

Eric was sucking his thumb. "When will we see you again?" I asked Cynthia as the bus appeared.

"I'll keep in touch," Cynthia said firmly, and hauled Sydney onto the bus.

We went slowly home under our burdens, and I fried fish for five people in the Woolworth frying pan. It took me an hour. The fish was delicious, although some of it got rather cold waiting for all of it to be fried in the one pan. We ate slowly, watching people's legs passing the kitchen window. It was raining.

7

Sheets

IN THE EVENING, we removed the sheets from our big bed and Jordan took them in a cab to the launderette where he spent the evening washing and drying them. Mark and I stayed home and watched television after Bruce and Eric went to bed.

"It's too bad your father is missing this play," I said to Mark.

The play was about a young man with long hair who lived in an elegant apartment and kept talking to a young woman with bangs. "My God, these Americans," the young man said. The girl sighed. "They're always talking about relating," the young man said. "How awful," the girl replied.

"What's this play about?" Mark asked.

"It's too early to tell," I said evasively. "But you know it's on the BBC."

We watched it a while longer. "I don't understand who keeps coughing," I said.

"I think it's the cameraman," Mark said.

The play ended when the young man and the young woman got married. Jordan returned with clean sheets just as a clergyman came on the screen to deliver a sermon. "They sign off with that," Jordan said. I found this surprising, because it was only eleven-twenty.

"You missed a swell play, Dad," Mark said, going up the stairs.

The next morning I was able to assure Mrs. Grail that we had clean sheets on the bed. "But they've never been aired," she said. I didn't know what that meant; it had a pleasantly archaic sound. "And how long can you keep it up?" she asked. "Him running about with them sheets, and them twisty rags on the boys' beds, and you without a frying pan. And all that rent."

I walked musing from the kitchen.

"I'll never get used to it, never," Mrs. Grail called after me. "Twenty-five years I've been here, and I'll never get used to it." I went upstairs where Jordan was dressing to leave for the office.

"I think you should call Mr. MacAllister about the sheets," I said. "No frying pan, and them twisty rags on the boys' beds. How long can you keep it up without an airing?"

"Well, I'll try," Jordan said. "Mr. MacAllister is an awfully nice guy, you know, I met him when I signed the lease. He lives in Belgravia." He dialed a number. After a while I heard a boiled sort of voice through the phone, screaming with laughter above the telephone noises, the wheezes and clicks and ghostly interruptions.

Jordan hung up with a pleased smile. "He *is* a nice guy. He said, 'Gone off to Scotland with the sheets, has she? Ha ha, how very like her. Go and buy the sheets and the frying pan and take it off the rent!'"

"I've already bought the frying pan," I said. "It cost eight shillings."

"Well, we'll take it off the rent," Jordan said. "He's a reasonable person. He can't help it if Mrs. Stackpole is a little eccentric." I went downstairs to report to Mrs. Grail. "Well, I certainly should buy them sheets," she said, "and new ones for the boys too. I never heard of such a thing. Sleeping on them rags. So he's the boyfriend, is he? And little children in the house."

"He's a reasonable person," I said. "He can't help it if Mrs. Stackpole is eccentric."

"Eccentric is it? I'm telling you it's the English, they'll do you every time. You run out and get them sheets, before she tells him off."

"How much do sheets cost?"

"They cost a lot," Mrs. Grail responded promptly. "Everything costs a lot in this benighted place. Oh, I've been here twenty-five years and I'll never get used to it, never. This Hoover is broken," she added, in a more conversational tone.

"Oh, what shall we do?" The thought of attempting to get anything repaired was almost too much for me. I had tried to buy a can opener and no one would sell it to me. They all said that you could get them free in pubs, but the pub people wouldn't give us one.

"Don't worry about it," Mrs. Grail said. "Blow it. Let her worry about it. I'll use a broom. This old thing," she said, kicking the vacuum cleaner. "It dates from the Ark. She hasn't a penny. Oh, I'll never get used to it, never."

"If the phone book had yellow pages," I said.

"Standing looking in a store window," Mrs. Grail said, bending over to puff up the sofa cushions in their chintz slip-cover, "and a woman edges up and bumps into me, 'Pardon me,' I says. 'Ah, go back,' she says, 'go back where you come from.' 'Yes,' I says, 'if the English will give us back our six counties,' I says, 'I'll go back where I come from.'"

"That woman was probably an eccentric," I said.

"'Go back where you come from,'" Mrs. Grail said, punching the cushion vigorously. "That's what they keep saying. My

husband's from the North, from Yorkshire, and the men he
works with, they tell him to go back where he come from."

"My goodness," I said.

"My Pat, those girls she works with, they mimic the way
she talks." She straightened up and brushed some lint off the
back of the sofa. "They hate Americans too," she said. "They
hate everybody. You'll find out." She paused dramatically in the
doorway, clutching the defunct Hoover. "Go get them sheets,"
she said. "I should hurry up if I was you."

Feeling rather shaken, I went down to the kitchen to calm
myself with a cup of coffee and the newspaper. Jordan had
originally ordered the *London Times* for me, but I found it less
than interesting, so he switched to the *Daily Telegraph.* I sipped
my instant coffee and read a review of the television play that
Mark and I had seen the night before.

"I do not know where these elegant kitchens come from
that one sees on these television dramas," the reviewer wrote
irascibly. "I certainly do not have one. I should like to make
it very clear that I would under no circumstances have such a
kitchen even if it were offered to me. We are being pervaded by
a pernicious materialism, most probably from across the sea."

8

Dr. Bott

ON SATURDAY MORNING we were awakened about eight
o'clock by a pounding on the door. I hurried down and, mindful of Mrs. Stackpole's warnings, called, "Who is it?"

"Telephone," a voice said.

I opened the door a crack and peered out into a sunny
Baldridge Place.

"We have a telephone," I said.

"This is for the attic," the man said. "To be installed. I have
to leave this cable here."

"What for?"

"I have to leave this cable here, to be installed at a later
date."

I stood aside reluctantly, and he clomped down to the
kitchen, dragging dirt and bits of fluff over Mrs. Stackpole's
impractical red hall carpeting.

"Waking us up," I said to Jordan. "Mrs. Stackpole never
mentioned it. She said her lodger was going to bring some
things to the attic one afternoon. Do you suppose that was a
burglar?"

"He wouldn't have all that cable with him if he was a burglar," Jordan said reasonably. He looked out the window. "The
sun's out," he remarked, in an awed voice.

After lunch Jane came with a friend named Tom and took Eric and Bruce to Hyde Park. Feeling quiet and peaceful, Jordan and Mark and I went to sit on folding chairs in Mrs. Stackpole's small but charming back garden. Paved in red brick and edged with flowers, it was surrounded with a ten-foot-high fence of wooden palings fastened together tightly and sharpened to murderous fangs all along the top.

"I don't think anyone could get in here," I said. "Why do we have to use all those burglar locks on the garden door?"

"I think Mrs. Stackpole is odd on the subject of locks," Jordan said.

We sat in the sun. I never sat in the sun at home; here I felt starved for sunlight. It had been gray and raining all week. The ground was very wet; the heat brought out huge black flies, and bees which hovered over the brilliant flowers. Steam rose around us.

"It's like a jungle out here," Mark said. He listened a moment as we sat stiffly on our folding chairs, our knees touching. A stillness pervaded everything. "Where *is* everybody?" he asked, nervously.

"It's quiet on Saturday afternoon in Knightsbridge," Jordan said. "All the shops are closed."

"Quiet!" Mark said. "I'll say it's quiet. Aren't there even any little kids?"

A ghostly sound of childish laughter floated through the air. Jordan rose and tried to peer through the fence palings, standing on tiptoe.

"How... old... are... you?" he called, in a high, lingering, eerie voice.

"I was ten..." Mark called back, "in eighteen fifty-six..."

We discovered that we were becoming rather depressed.

"I'm supposed to go to Battersea with Vincent," Mark said. Vincent was one of Jordan's employees: he was fifteen, the same age as Mark and vaguely Asian in appearance.

"That's nice, dear," I said, pleased that my boy had made a friend. Mark went off in the general direction of the Knightsbridge Underground station.

"Let's take a walk," Jordan said brightly.

I don't normally drink, except at parties, but I said that I really thought I could use a drink.

"You can't be served for an hour or two," Jordan said apologetically.

We went into the house, which was cold and damp, and locked all the windows and the French door with the little black and gold keys that Mrs. Stackpole had left us for this purpose. There were four locks on the French door alone. Luckily the sun was still shining when we emerged into the street. We walked slowly toward the square. Children were playing in the little gated private park.

We paused and stared over the iron fence. "Listen, our kids could play with those children there," Jordan said, becoming excited.

I felt an odd doubt. "We haven't got a key," I said.

"Dr. Bott will have one," Jordan said. "He lives right over there, across the square—didn't I tell you about Dr. Bott? He's awfully nice. I went to him with my knee, and when I burnt my hand..."

"But..." I said.

"Good old Dr. Bott," Jordan said fondly. He began to move toward the row of houses on the opposite side of the square.

I hung back. "Let's not," I said. "I don't want to ask him."

"Don't be silly," Jordan said testily. "You don't know him." He mounted the steep stairs. "He'll be delighted to help," he said, and rang, or pulled, the bell.

"Nobody's home," I said hastily, and began to back down the steps.

"Someone's coming," Jordan said. "What's wrong with you?" The red door opened, and a man with fair hair stood before us. He stared blankly at Jordan through protuberant blue eyes.

"Yes?" he said coldly.

"Dr. Bott!" Jordan cried jovially. I turned and went hastily down the stairs. "Are you busy?" Jordan said. A note of hesitation crept into his voice.

"Yes," Dr. Bott said, lifting his upper lip in what could only be described as a snarl. "I'm afraid I am." By this time I had reached the pavement and was heading for the Brompton Road. "Wife," Jordan was babbling, "family... here... visit...." I glanced over my shoulder and saw Dr. Bott smiling at me.

"What!" he called, "All the way from America?"

"Yes," I called back, using his favorite word, and hotfooted it down the empty street. I waited for Jordan at the corner. He appeared shortly, with a peculiar expression on his face. "Good old Dr. Bott," I said.

"He said he wanted some time with his family," Jordan said. "'I'd like *some* time with my family, you know,' was the way he put it."

"How did he know we didn't want medical help?"

"He didn't. He didn't ask me what we wanted."

We walked through the empty streets, holding hands, and staring with unseeing eyes into shop windows. Finally we had some coffee and then we went home, and Jordan began writing letters, all beginning "My dear Dr. Bott..."

Bruce and Eric came home. They said all they had done in the park was lie on the grass while Jane rubbed Tom's back. Then they went on lying in the grass and Tom rubbed Jane's back.

We turned on the television set, but the only thing on both stations (there were only two) was Harold Wilson going in and out of Ten Downing Street. A Commonwealth Conference had started. The children played checkers; Mrs. Stackpole's glass curtains stirred in the breeze. It occurred to me that it was the middle of June, and that if we were home the children would be out riding their bicycles or swimming at the beach, but I pushed that thought away.

After a while, Mark returned, looking annoyed. He said Vincent didn't have any money, so he shared all his money with Vincent, and then when all his money was gone except his carfare, Vincent called him selfish. He said that since Mark was the son of an American millionaire, he had to be lying when he said that all he had left was carfare.

"Vincent's an idiot," Jordan said.

Our Saturday ended with a trip in a cab to a delicatessen in South Kensington where we purchased goodies for dinner and for the next day, when Jane and her mother and brothers were coming to tea.

9

Liz and Jane

THE NEXT DAY being Sunday, we all had a leisurely breakfast together, consisting of eggs from the Woolworth frying pan, and toast made under the broiler, one piece lifted by fork every three minutes. I piled the chipped mismatched dishes and glasses in the dish drainer to dry cloudily, and thought about my old electric dishwasher at home. For years I had complained about machine civilization and life in the wasteland of materialism: now I felt a subtle change taking place in me. Henry James was being replaced by Buckminster Fuller.

I shoved twelve or thirteen of Mrs. Stackpole's blanket and linen layers into place on our oversized bed and got dressed shortly before the doorbell rang. Descending, I found the eight-by-ten-foot sitting room bulging with people in t-shirts and blue jeans.

Jane was there with her friend Tom and several of her brothers, all with long bangs or fringes, and her mother Liz, a rather paunchy lady with orange hair and fingernails, who was wearing a green silk print blouse, a tight red wool skirt, and blue high-heeled shoes. After effusive greetings, we went down to the kitchen where we ate little sandwiches I had prepared, and drank tea. Mrs. Stackpole, incredibly, had left only a small teapot, and Jordan had had to buy a larger one. Jane stopped me when I was about to put the leftovers into the refrigerator.

"Silly old cow," she said to me affectionately. Liz wrapped them all carefully in aluminum foil, put them into two large tin cookie boxes and put the boxes in a drawer in the dresser. I had noticed this aversion to the refrigerator in Mrs. Grail, who unfailingly placed milk and butter on the hutch shelves and asked me whether I wanted to put unopened cans of soup in *there*, pointing with distaste to the refrigerator. This distrust of refrigeration probably explained the rich aroma of sour milk I had frequently encountered. Anyway, after Liz had disposed of the little sandwiches, we decided to walk to Hyde Park, because it was a lovely sunny day.

Liz and I sat primly on a bench while Jordan and the young things leapt gaily over the grass. Jane at one point dashed for a ball and fell heavily to the ground, where she remained, rubbing her leg.

"Oh, dear," I said, "she's hurt herself."

"Yes," Liz said. "She does try to do too much."

Jane continued to sit rubbing her leg, while Jordan and Tom hung over her, looking concerned.

"We can't all be athletes," I said.

"Everybody loves Jane," Liz said, responding instantly to something in my tone. "Everybody that knows her is just wild about her."

"Eric loves her," I said, after a moment.

"Everybody does," Liz said firmly. "And Jane expects that. She expects that everyone will love her."

I began to feel that I had failed Jane.

"She and Jordan are very close," Liz said. "She wants to take care of Jordan." An icy wind blew across the grassy plain of the park. I was wearing a coat over my sweater, but my ears began to tingle, and I noticed that Liz's lips matched her shoes. "Shall we take a walk?" I asked. "It's getting chilly."

"It does get cold sometimes in the summer," Liz said defensively.

We began to stroll slowly toward the sidewalk, or pavement.

"Jordan is so brave," Liz said, "and so likeable. Coming all the way over here alone, to start a business the way he did."

"Yes, he's very brave; he—"

"And Bill," Liz said, referring to Bill Dworkin. "Bill Dorking. He's such a gentleman. He even *sounds* like a gentleman. He sounds English."

"That's the way they talk in New Jersey," I said.

"Do they? Well, he sounds English to me. I think he speaks beautifully."

We strolled a little farther, in silence. The London Hilton came into view.

"There's the London Hilton," Liz said. "Don't you think it's horrible?"

"Well," I said.

"Everybody feels it spoils the park. American structure spoiling the park. You can see it, right from here."

"Oh, you can see it all right," I said.

"I'm so fond of Bill," Liz said. "Jordan is lucky to have him. He's so gentle. English people understand that, being quiet, you know, and a gentleman. Sometimes I would like to tell Jordan that one really needs to be a restrained sort of person to succeed here in business. One needs to be quiet to be accepted. More like Bill."

"Oh, you really should tell Jordan that," I said. "He'd be so grateful."

"A lot of push doesn't go here, you know," Liz said gently. "You'll find it's different here from America." I said that I had noticed that it was different. "Of course," Liz went on, "that's all right. You shouldn't mind. We're five hundred years ahead of you, you see. We've had more time to become civilized."

I looked at her, speechless.

"You can't catch up with us, you know," Liz said. "But don't worry, in five hundred years things will be different in America." After the ensuing pause, she asked, "What do people think about us in America? What do American people think about the English?"

I said that everybody thought I was very fortunate to be able to come for the summer.

At this point the active members of our group signaled defeat in the face of the rising wind, and we went home, walking close to brick walls whenever we could, for shelter. We descended to the basement again, opened the drawers to get the little sandwiches out of the cookie tins and the aluminum foil, and brewed more tea. Everybody was animated, except me. I was thinking about what Liz had said, and wondering why she had said it. Finally our visitors departed, much to my relief.

We turned on the television, to relax for a few minutes. There was a thing on called *Mystery Theatre*. The camera circled constantly, up and down staircases, and people poured whiskey out of decanters while the camera crew kept clearing their throats and occasionally there was a loud crash; otherwise nothing much happened. We noticed it was over when credits began to travel down the screen.

At about ten-thirty, a clergyman appeared, in a very close close-up, and told a little story about an old lady who wrote to the bishop for groceries and then sat in the living room near the window and waited for him until she fell asleep. In the meantime, the bishop had come in through the back door and left the groceries on the kitchen table. The point of this story seemed to be that a lot of us sit in the front room when we should really be in the kitchen. Or something like that. We discussed the point of this parable until "God Save the Queen" was played while the screen showed us a portrait of the Queen in evening dress before it went blank and silent. We hauled ourselves up, feeling very tired indeed, and suddenly a jolly voice came out of the dead set. "You won't forget to turn it off, will you?" it asked kindly. So we turned it off.

10

Sightseeing and Shopping

ON MONDAY we were awakened very early by another telephone man; this one brought several hundred yards of cable into the kitchen and left it there.

"The tenant was only supposed to come one afternoon," I said to Mrs. Grail, when she arrived at ten.

"Well, they'll do you, you know," she said. "Every time." Her voice dropped. "I saw her this morning," she said. "In Knightsbridge."

"Who?"

"Mrs. Stackpole. I saw her this morning. In the Knightsbridge Road."

"But she's in Scotland."

"Ah, she never is. I saw her this morning, the same blue skirt and that sweater. I'd know her anywhere." She gave a rather creepy glance at the windows. "She's staying somewhere here, close by."

The phone rang and Jordan answered it upstairs. I excused myself and joined him; I could hear Mr. MacAllister's boiled voice shrieking through the receiver. It didn't sound good.

"No sheets," I said, when he hung up.

"He says he's been on to her. And she was very upset, about the sheets and the frying pan and all that. She said no linens and I said what about human decency, but he didn't seem to know what I meant. He said we could leave if we didn't like it."

"Well, what did she say about sheets when you rented the place?"

"I can't remember," Jordan said sheepishly. "I remember thinking it was all right."

I looked moodily out the window. "Mrs. Grail said she saw her today, in the Knightsbridge Road. She says she's staying here somewhere, spying on us."

"That's ridiculous," he said briskly. "What would she want to do that for?"

I shrugged.

"Well, have a good day," he said hastily, and set off with Mark for the bus. We had decided to spend the afternoon enjoying the local sights. Jordan had suggested we walk through Knightsbridge to the Victoria and Albert Museum.

"You're going out?" Mrs. Grail asked. She looked around nervously. "It's so quiet here without the boys," she said. "And that damn clock ticking."

"Well, we want to see a few things," I said brightly. It was a relatively mild day; we were comfortable with sweaters under our raincoats. The sky was gray and threatening, but it was not raining. We walked along for several blocks. Bruce kept saying that we were lost. "It's too far," he said. "There isn't any museum. It's the wrong way. My feet hurt."

Finally we found it, huge and gray, dark gray. I went boldly up to the desk. The lady sitting there looked alarmed. "You ought to go to the Children's Museum at Bethnal Green," she said. "We haven't anything for children here."

I had no idea how to get to Bethnal Green. "Haven't you *anything?*" I asked.

"Well, there's the armor."

"Oh, armor!" I cried, beaming at my charges, "Oh, good! You'll love the armor. Where is it?"

"Well, you walk through the Church Plate…"

We walked through the Church Plate, cheerfully discussing it, and eventually found the armor.

"Oh, look!" I called gaily. "Oh, my goodness, Bruce, look at this big shield!"

"Oh!" Bruce cried. "Isn't it big? My goodness, you mean they really carried that?"

"Indeed they did," I said. "Doesn't it look heavy? My goodness…"

"Oh, look!" Eric cried. "Look at this big sword!"

"Oh, goodness!" I cried back. "Look, Bruce!"

After about ten minutes of this, I was going on about a large iron gauntlet, when Eric spoke in a low, despairing voice.

"Let's get out of here," he said.

Silently, we slunk past the Church Plate and out into the street. A light rain was falling, and it was cold. We went to a little restaurant and ordered hamburgers. They came, gray slabs of meat in a square metal dish, covered with greasy gravy. No bread. And the milk was warm.

"We'll go to Harrods," I said cheerfully, "and I'll buy something delicious for dinner. And we'll look around Harrods."

So we trudged to Harrods, and we looked around. Everything seemed very expensive; prices seemed to have doubled since Jordan and I had come to London as tourists, two years before. Finally we went down into the food halls. I gathered up my courage and approached the meat counter. A woman in a white coat was sitting on a high stool behind the roasts, chewing on something.

Using my tentative polite approach, I edged in a few feet to the left of her, eyeing her with my right eye, and clearing my throat hopefully. She chewed on, staring straight before her. I edged a few inches closer to her line of vision and said, "Uh…"

She glanced at me irritably and said, "Oh, move along, madam, move along. Get down to the end of the counter. Get away!"

"Well!" I said, gasping.

"Oh, get away," she responded.

I moved down to the end of the counter, still gasping, and a meek butcher cut a roast for me. The woman in the white coat sat glaring at me during the entire transaction. "What a rude woman!" I said to the butcher. He smiled at me meekly. Apparently, I had blundered into her tea break.

Gathering up my roast, I sailed with my little tykes toward the exit in the drug department. Near Drugs was Hairbrushes. Bruce and I each needed a hairbrush. Surprised to discover that English hairbrushes cost more in London than in Chicago, I weighed two in my hand while I thought about it. "If you can't decide, it's better to leave it," the saleswoman said coldly. "We close in ten minutes."

I put the hairbrushes down and we exited through Drugs.

11

Further Adventures

THE NEXT DAY two telephone men came, hollering to each other as they dragged rubbery coils around. Mrs. Grail complained to me bitterly. I responded that I really couldn't see why all this should go on. "It was only supposed to take an afternoon for her to move in."

"Ah, that's the way of them," Mrs. Grail said. "That's the British for you. She'll have it nice and easy when she comes in September and you've had all the mess and all the aggravation. And I've swept down them stairs three times already and they've tracked in all the mud. And now you can't get the sheets, and them twisty rags on the boys' beds. I wouldn't put them in a kennel. And you paying all that rent."

"A woman yelled at me in Harrods yesterday," I said moodily. "At the meat counter."

"Oh, I've been here twenty-five years," Mrs. Grail said. "And I'll never get used to it. Never."

"The children are holding up very well, though," I said. "My husband and I were discussing it yesterday. Well, Bruce's stomach is upset—maybe the milk is too rich—but Eric is doing well. He's such a good traveler. We've taken him to Wisconsin and Boston and Maine and never a bit of trouble with him. He loves to travel."

"Ah, the dear little tyke," Mrs. Grail said.

"He's kind of fresh, though," I said.

"Ah, they're all awful," Mrs. Grail said. "I had four of them and I love them dearly, but if I had it to do over again, I wouldn't have any. I'm a Catholic but you've got to use common sense. They're all a great trial."

"Well," I said. "Anyway, Eric seems to take it all in his stride."

"The dear little thing," Mrs. Grail said. "But why do they like the Beatles so much? I can't stand them, but Elvis Presley is lovely, isn't he?"

"Yes, he is," I said, measuring out drops for Bruce's stomach. "I think I'll take them to Madame Tussaud's today. The Victoria and Albert wasn't good."

"Oh, they'll love Madame Tussaud's. You go out here to Knightsbridge and take a Number Nine bus..." We gathered ourselves together and straggled off in the rain, leaving Mrs. Grail wrapped around the doorpost, her eyes begging us not to leave her alone in the house.

Madame Tussaud's seemed to be a success; the children waited quietly in the long lines before every exhibit. Eric looked nervously at the image of the Queen Mother; its eyes were glittering strangely under the lights.

"Who's *that?*" he cried, pointing.

"It's the Queen Mother, dear," I said loudly. "She's an awfully nice lady."

They wanted to go to the Chamber of Horrors, and on the way we stopped in the Diorama Room before the diorama of Hamlet. Hamlet was standing on a stony platform, and the Ghost loomed in the background. "Do you see that?" I said, showing off. "That's Hamlet, and that's the ghost of Hamlet's father, and he's telling Hamlet that Hamlet's uncle Claudius murdered him by dropping poison in his ear and..."

After I finished giving a summary of the play, we went on down to the Chamber of Horrors which the boys seemed to like. When we got home, I cooked hamburgers in an electric frying pan that I had found hidden in a cupboard in the laundry room. It was rather greasy, but I washed it thoroughly, plugged it in, and it worked.

The next morning we received a letter from Mrs. Stackpole. She seemed angry because of the Great Sheet Controversy and repeated the point of view delivered to us by Mr. MacAllister. "As for the frying pan," she wrote, "I am terribly sorry not to have provided one, but I am afraid that is an object I *never* use!" There was a good deal more in the same vein. Shortly after we finished reading the letter, the telephone rang. Jordan spoke genially for a few minutes, and then hung up. "It's Miss Pip," he said. "The lodger. She wants to bring a few things in. I told her someone would be here until two o'clock, so don't forget to tell Mrs. Grail."

"They've already driven us crazy with the telephone," I said, "dragging dust and fluff all over the stairs, and them twisty bits of rag…"

"Well, we said she could move a few things in," Jordan said reasonably.

I took the children to see a Jerry Lewis movie in Piccadilly. It was in color: we watched the California sun beat down on everyone, and it was an adjustment emerging into the gray London streets.

"Let's go and have a nice lunch," I said enthusiastically. "We'll go to Fortnum's Fountain Bar." This had been recommended to me as one of the best places in the city for lunch.

We established ourselves at the bar and tried to attract the attention of the waitress, who was lounging against the counter, chatting with a blond chinless youth. "I really hate it here," she was saying. "The kitchen is filthy."

I cleared my throat.

"Are you going to Boopsie's on Saturday?" the waitress asked wistfully. The youth said he was thinking of it. "I wish I could go," she said. "I'm so exhausted all the time. It's so difficult here, and the other girls…"

"How about some scrambled eggs?" I asked Eric, who sat droopily beside me, his chin resting on the counter.

"I'm not hungry," he said faintly.

"You haven't had anything to eat all day," I said, puzzled. "See? It says here, 'Scrambled Eggs, Prawns, on Toast with Green Salad'… You don't like prawns or salad, so we'll just have the eggs and toast. Doesn't that sound good?"

"All right," he said.

"I want the stuffed Canadian bacon with cheese sauce," Bruce said. He fell off his stool, which collapsed on top of him. Eric continued staring moodily into space. I climbed down and helped Bruce up, righting his chair.

"I want to go home," Bruce said.

"If I *am* able to go to Boopsie's on Saturday…" the waitress was saying.

"Miss," the woman sitting next to Eric said apologetically, "I'm afraid my lobster's full of sand."

"I'll be back in a minute," the waitress said reluctantly to her friend. She turned to the woman next to me, inspected her lobster, and agreed that it was full of sand.

"Could you take our order?" I asked.

"One moment," she replied frostily, and went off with the sandy lobster.

"I never had sandy lobster before," the woman said to me. She was a compatriot of ours, and very embarrassed about making a fuss. Another waitress came up to us. "Yes?" she asked.

"He wants the Canadian bacon with cheese sauce," I said. "And he wants the scrambled eggs. Can he have it without prawns, please?"

"We don't have scrambled eggs," the waitress said.

"Yes, you do," I replied. Eric sat drearily next to me, his chin still on the counter. "Here," I said, pointing to the menu. "Scrambled eggs and Prawns on Toast, with Green Salad."

"Oh, scrambled eggs with *prawns,*" the waitress said. "Yes, we have that."

"Can he have it without prawns, please?"

There was a pause.

"All you have to do is take the prawns off," I said encouragingly.

She hesitated. Finally she made a decision.

"I can take the prawns off," she said firmly, "but you'll have to have the green salad." "All right," I said. "We can push it aside," I whispered to Eric, who was still staring moodily into space.

When the eggs came, on toast, with the green salad, I was relieved to see him tuck it in with good appetite. Bruce was enjoying the Canadian bacon. Eric dug the toast out from under the eggs, ate it, and asked for another piece.

The waitress hesitated again.

"We do *do* toast," she said. "But I don't know if you can *have* toast. With that," she added. "I'll go and check." Eric sighed. In less than twenty minutes, she was back, triumphant, bearing a plate of sliced, buttered tea toast. Eric consumed it, still moodily.

But that night, he didn't touch his dinner. "What's wrong?" Mark asked him.

"I want to go home!" Eric said, and before our horrified eyes, he dropped his head on the table and began to sob. "I'm afraid of King Claudius! I want to go home!"

A dull cloud of gloom descended over the kitchen.

"Let's all go upstairs and watch television," Jordan said heartily. "We'll see what's on."

Puppets appeared on the screen. One was lying on a stretcher, moaning and sobbing as he was being pushed through swinging doors. "Oh, oh, oh!" he shrieked. "Don't take me to the hospital, don't, don't! I'm afraid, I'm afraid of the hospital!" Another door opened and another puppet, decidedly African in appearance, swathed in a long white medical gown, approached the screaming sufferer. He was holding a huge hypodermic needle, nearly as long as his leg. The camera shot him from below, so that he appeared to be very tall. "Ho ho ho!" he said. "I am the doctor. I am going to stick you with this needle."

"Oh no!" howled the sufferer, who had great goggly eyes and resembled a frog. "Oh don't! Oh, I'm frightened of the hospital! I'm frightened of the doctor! Oh, please, please don't! Oh—!"

The enormous puppet approached, raising the needle. The toad on the stretcher went into a frenzy of screams. Mark broke the frozen spell in which we sat, crawled over to the set and turned it off. "My God!" he said. Eric turned to me with a weak smile. "That was Sammy Snake," he said. My flat American voice rose in the cold, chintzy, mildewed air of 16 Baldrige Place. "Doctors are our friends," I said. Jordan did not meet my eyes.

12

Miss Pip

THE NEXT DAY Mrs. Grail bustled in, full of news and indignation. 'That creature turned up," she said. "You never told me she was coming." I had already realized that I had forgotten to tell Mrs. Grail about Miss Pip, who had phoned Jordan, full of complaints about Mrs. Grail.

"Here the doorbell rings," Mrs. Grail said, "And me all alone in the house, and here is a dreadful creature on the stoop, a man. Ah, the face on him." She shuddered. "And the coat! So I wouldn't let them in. You never told me. And here she comes. Ah, the creature! And they wouldn't go away. So I slammed the door in their faces. But they rang and rang. So I let them in, but I followed them all about. Tracking dirt and fluff, up and down the stairs, carting bits and pieces."

"They're coming back today," I told her.

"I know," Mrs. Grail said grimly. "The creatures. And they're never married, are they?"

"I doubt it," I said primly. "She's taken the rooms alone, I think. I'm sure that's what Mrs. Stackpole said."

"Oh, yes. Alone. And then the monkeyshines start! Probably asked to leave her other rooms, I shouldn't wonder."

"My husband told them you'd only be here until two. So just let them in today."

We had grown weary of rushing our two sheets off the big bed to the launderette where Jordan went in a cab and spent the evening, invariably missing the only good TV programs that were ever on. "I'm going to call a laundry," I announced to Mrs. Grail. "While the sheets are out, we'll use that funny-looking embroidered thing and that other funny thin blanket instead."

"Ah, that's right," she said. "I should force them to give you sheets but if they won't, just use them bits and pieces off the bed. More bits and pieces on this bed. Look at that," she said, kicking a drooping ruffle.

I examined Mrs. Stackpole's list. "Here's a laundry," I said.

"Don't call *her* laundry. Call the Sunlight Laundry. Ah, they're lovely."

I called the Sunlight Laundry off and on all morning and got a busy signal each time. I decided to call the general operator. "It must be out of order," I told her. "It's a place of business. A laundry."

"Just a minute, dear," the operator said. She called another operator. There were a lot of clickings and buzzings.

"It's engaged," the second operator said.

"She says it's a laundry, dear," the first operator remarked.

"Oh, a laundry?" the second operator asked.

"It's been engaged all morning," the first operator told her.

"Well, just a minute, dear," the second operator said. "I'll look into it."

"Oh, thank you, dear," the first operator said. "She's just looking into it," she assured me.

"Okay," I said. I didn't mind waiting; I was reading a book. After a while the second operator returned. "It's out of order, dear," she said, apparently to the first operator.

"Oh, is it? Thank you so much, dear."

"Well, not at all, dear. That's all right."

"Goodbye, dear."

"Goodbye."

The first operator came back to me. "It's out of order, dear," she said, unnecessarily.

"How long will it take to fix it?"

Her voice lost some of its good humor. "Well, I don't know, dear. A day or two. Maybe three. It's hard to say. It depends what's wrong with it. It's out of order, you see. It's not working."

By this time it was a quarter of two and time for us to be on our way, wandering aimlessly about London, looking for toilets for Bruce and Eric, whose stomachs were upset, possibly from the rich milk.

"I'm all through now," Mrs. Grail said. "What about them creatures?"

"It's ten minutes of two. If they were coming, they wouldn't come this late. They know you leave at two."

We all bundled into raincoats and gloves and scarves and opened the front door. On the stoop stood what were unquestionably the two creatures: a very tall, very thin girl with long red hair and a horrified expression, and a shorter, thicker male, wearing a cardboard-looking checked jacket and wild curls.

"Yes?" I said.

"Mrs. Miller?" the girl said.

"Yes," I said.

"Are you going out?" the girl asked, her look of horror deepening.

"Yes," I said, adding, so as not to sound like Dr. Bott, "I am."

"But it's not two o'clock yet. Your husband said there would be someone here until two."

"It's six minutes of."

There was a silence. They stood on the stoop, staring at us with aversion and terror, and we crowded sloppily in the doorway, a welter of scarves and coats, caps and umbrellas, un-English and undisciplined.

"Don't you want to come in?" I asked.

"We did want to bring in a few things, yes," Miss Pip said, for I had to assume this was she.

"Well, we'll wait for you." We all, including Mrs. Grail, went into the sitting room and sat down, in our coats. Miss Pip and her nameless friend rushed up and down the stairs, carrying small shabby objects. They rushed frantically, silently, poker-faced. Mrs. Grail perched on the edge of Mrs. Stackpole's fat-armed sofa and murmured to me insidiously. "This is the second trip. And the telephone men. Ah, you're too soft with them. I shouldn't allow it."

"Mrs. Stackpole told me—one afternoon to bring in a few things," I replied, working myself into a rage. "She didn't say anything about the telephone men. And *two* afternoons."

"And all the money," Mrs. Grail said. "And the washing machine. And them twisty rags. And no sheets to your bed. Ah God, it's the English, they'll do you every time."

Miss Pip and her friend came downstairs, still looking upset, and stood facing us near the tiny entrance hall. We all rose. "Thank you very much," Miss Pip said, staring into my eyes with an expression of disbelief. "We've finished."

"Fine," I said. She continued to stand before the hall entrance, not moving.

'The decorator," she said, "the man who is making my curtains for the windows in the apartment upstairs... He is supposed to meet us here."

There was a long pause.

"I told him to be here at two," Miss Pip said.

"It's a quarter after now," I said.

"I know," she responded. "He's late."

"We have to go out," I said.

"He has to measure the windows," she said.

I felt Mrs. Grail's eyes boring into the back of my neck.

"Look," I said. "This is really ridiculous. Mrs. Stackpole told me you would come in one afternoon to bring in a few things, but the telephone men have been here about four times, waking us up and tracking dirt, and now you've come *twice* and you make appointments with people… I know it's not your fault." I added, "Mrs. Stackpole misled me, but we are paying quite a lot of rent, and it's our home for the summer, and I do think this is ridiculous."

"I can see you're very angry," Miss Pip said.

"I really think we all ought to go now," I said.

"I promised to meet the man here."

"Well, he isn't here," I said, feeling like a rat, "and we really have to go out now. Mrs. Grail leaves at two, anyway. My husband told you that. And if I wasn't here, you would have delayed her." Miss Pip continued to stand in the hall doorway and stare at me with wide shocked eyes. "I think we ought to go," I said, enunciating distinctly. Mrs. Grail and Bruce and Eric crowded up behind me and began to move forward. "I expect the man at any moment," Miss Pip said, not moving. "I can see you're very angry."

I could feel Mrs. Grail's eyes.

"We'll just stay here and wait for him," Miss Pip said. "You can go."

"I don't know if Mrs. Stackpole would like me to do that," I said, remembering all the locks and keys....

"We'll just stand in the hall," Miss Pip said. "We won't touch the wall. We won't touch anything." This was such an outrageous remark that I capitulated.

"Oh, you can't stand in the hall," I said. "Come in, sit down. Wait for him."

We edged past them, Indian file, and went out in silence. On the way to the bus I kept trying to justify my behavior to Mrs. Grail. I knew I had failed; I didn't know whether I had been too unkind or not unkind enough. Later I was to think about Miss Pip's persistence. It was a quality she shared with Mrs. Stackpole and Mr. MacAllister. These people were not to be put off. The Fuzzy Wuzzies, the East Indians, and Mrs. Grail's ancestors, among others, had found it very difficult to put them off. By nature less positive than they, what chance had I?

13

Help in Sight

AFTER SEVERAL cold and rainy days spent trying to find something for Bruce and Eric to do, I decided to phone the American Embassy. Everybody who spoke to me there sounded English.

"I have these three children," I said, when I was connected with the apparently appropriate voice. "Three, but only the two younger ones present a problem. I have to find something for them to do. Can you suggest something for them to do during the day? Anything."

"Well, I can't really," the voice said, through its nose.

"You mean there isn't anything?"

"Well, there used to be a teenage club at the American Air Force base in West Ruyslip, but it's been discontinued."

"Oh, well, the teenager is relatively easy..."

"You might call the American Air Force base, but I'm afraid they discontinued the club. Still, you might try."

"I'll try anything," I said.

A male voice, vaguely Midwestern, answered at the Air Force base. I fought back an impulse to sob. He connected me with a recreation center, where a very Texan lady responded.

"... and I have these three children," I said, "but only two of them present a problem. And the woman at the Embassy said you had a teenage program, but you discontinued it, and she said you didn't have anything else."

"That's not true," the Texas voice said.

"The woman at the Embassy," I said.

"She didn't tell you the truth," the voice said bitterly. "We have a teenage club and we have a pre-teen day camp."

"You have a pre-teen day camp?"

"Yes, we do. We have a pre-teen day camp and it's open to civilians and all you have to do is get them here at nine o'clock. It runs from nine to four, every other week all summer."

"Do you have a bus service?"

"No, you have to get them here. I don't know exactly how you'd manage all the way from Knightsbridge."

"I'll manage," I said fervently. "I'll get them there."

I called Jordan at the office. "How are things going?" I asked.

"Uh," he said.

"Well, anyway, the American Air Force has a day camp at West Ruyslip from nine to four every other week. All I have to do is get them there."

"Great," Jordan said. "Wonderful."

"How do I get them there?"

"Call the minicab people. They'll drive them out there every day."

"Won't that be expensive?"

"No, it won't. Do you mind if I call you back later? Bill went to the bank to get the payroll money and they're holding him there because there isn't any payroll money."

"Do you mean they're holding him prisoner?"

"No," he said irritably, "of course they're not holding him prisoner. They're just holding him. Can I call you back?"

I should mention that at that time it was customary for English companies to pay their employees in cash. Every week Bill went to the bank, cashed a check for the full amount of the payroll and then got five- and one-pound notes, ten shilling notes, plus a certain number of half crowns, two shilling pieces, shillings, threepenny bits and pence. The resulting heavy brown paper package was brought back to the office; the contents were spread out on Bill's desk and counted into little pay packets for each of the thirty employees. The whole process took more or less half a day. Jordan had asked the staff if they would take checks instead of cash, but they wouldn't consider that.

I phoned the minicab people; the man said going back and forth to West Ruyslip by cab would be too expensive. But, heartened by the knowledge that help existed, I decided to take another stab at finding a laundry. After their phone service had been restored, I had called the Sunlight Laundry every few days, and each time someone at the laundry told me something. Sometimes they told me they came to Knightsbridge on Thursdays; other times they told me they came to Knightsbridge on Mondays; sometimes they told me to call back when the manager was in; and there were times when they told me they did not come to Knightsbridge at all. Today, feeling happy about the day camp, I called a different laundry and made arrangements for Tuesdays, when they seemed to feel they could come to Knightsbridge.

Elated, I flew downstairs to where the children sat listening to Beatles records. "Good news," I said. "The American Air Force base at West Ruyslip has a day camp every day from nine to four every other week." Eric looked at me blankly. His mind, I hoped, was on the Beatles and not Hamlet's uncle.

"I'm not going," Bruce said.

"You have to go," I said. "It's lots of fun. They have—"

"I'm not going," Bruce said. "Why do I have to go? I don't want to go. I hate camp."

"They have games and excursions, all sorts of thing," I said.

"I hate camp," Bruce said. "You know I hate camp. You made me go to camp last summer and I broke my toe."

"We'll discuss it later," I said.

"There's nothing to discuss," Bruce said. "What is there to discuss?"

I went upstairs to the bedroom and closed the door. I was reading when Bruce came in.

"I was glad I broke my toe last summer," he said. "That's how much I hated camp. I'll break something else if you make me go."

"We'll discuss it later," I said.

"I refuse to go to camp," Bruce said. "It's a horrible baby camp. Eric and I will be together, it will be horrible. I'll have to do what the babies do."

"You don't know whether that's true, and anyway there's nothing else for you to do," I said, dialing the office.

"I could work for Dad," Bruce said, "like Mark does. But oh, no, I have to keep Eric company. Now you want me to keep Eric company in camp."

"Hello?" I said. "How's everything? Did Bill get out?"

"Yes," Jordan said. "Basil Goldbrick had to go down and sign for him. I think Basil Goldbrick is going to buy into the company. It's either that or curtains."

"How would you feel about curtains?" I asked.

"I would consider curtains," he said.

"Everybody will hate me there," Bruce said. "I'm not going and that's all."

"How would you feel about dinner out?" I said. "I seem to feel a headache coming on."

"Oh, I suppose that's my fault you have a headache," Bruce said. "I suppose if I refuse to go to camp everyone in the house will hate me forever."

"Okay," Jordan said. "Who's that talking?"

When he and Mark came home, we ate in Knightsbridge, at a restaurant fitted up like the Roman catacombs. All the waiters were Spanish and friendly, and wore short tunics. They were generally muscular, and the place was very agreeable, except for the food. After dinner we emerged into a warm dusk. As we crossed the street, an irate taxi driver grew tired of waiting for us to troop by, and edged forward, nudging Jordan with his fender.

"Hey," Jordan said. "Watch it."

The driver became agitated and leaned largely out of his cab window, saying terrible things in a very loud voice. "Calm down," Jordan said to the cab driver.

"Look out," I said. "He's getting out. He'll punch you."

"Rude drivers," Jordan said; we followed him rapidly to the other side of the street.

We always crossed streets rapidly in London. Encroaching traffic was frightening. Every time we started to walk somewhere, Bruce asked, "Do we have to cross the street?" "I don't know what's wrong with these people," I said."Why are they so homicidal? Every time I have to cross a street, I feel faint."

"Cross at the zebra," Jordan said. He was referring to pedestrian crossings marked on the pavement by diagonal white lines.

"But you don't know whether they'll stop."

"They won't if you look hesitant."

"But they're required to by law," I said. "I thought they were so law-abiding. Why do they stay in queues until the bus comes and then shove and push and step all over each other?"

"Stop knocking everything," Mark said.

"You know I'm an Anglophile," I replied.

We were approaching the offices of the Playboy Club, which also doubled as living quarters for Victor Lownes, Playboy's London manager. Mark peered down into the area. "Gosh," he said. "Look at that modern kitchen. Look at the stainless steel."

"Stop looking in windows," I said.

"But it's so cheerful," Mark said. "Look, it's all new. It's clean."

"Come on," I said. Suddenly something hit me on the head.

"Something hit me on the head," I said.

"What do you mean?" Jordan said.

"Something soft," I said. I looked up. A blonde woman stood on a low balcony over our heads. She grasped the rail with both hands and looked into my eyes; her expression was inscrutable.

"She dropped something on my head," I said, pointing upward. We all looked up except Eric, who was dancing a jig at the end of the street. The woman stared back at us with gleaming eyes. We remained frozen for a moment, in a kind of tableau, and then we moved on, confused.

"Are you sure she dropped something?" Jordan asked.

When we entered the moldy entrance hall of 16 Baldridge Place, I found large bread crumbs and a piece of crust on my coat collar.

"She dropped bread on my head," I said, awed.

"She must have thought you were a bird," Jordan said.

Mark said, "I don't understand why these things keep happening to you."

14

Flood

THE NEXT MORNING it suddenly began to rain much more heavily than usual. It was a storm: water gushed, huge hailstones fell rattling onto the little balcony outside our bedroom window. "Ah, God," Mrs. Grail called up to me, "come down and look. Ah, God."

In the basement, the hall between the kitchen and the laundry room was ankle deep in muddy water. "Look at that," Mrs. Grail said with gloomy satisfaction. "The place is falling apart. Ah, they'll die here in the winter; they will, they'll die of cold. She hasn't spent a winter here yet, you know. Look at the walls."

It was true: our charming little old town house appeared to be moldering and even crumbling in spots. It had certainly been tinkered with: wires and pipes swooped in and out of the walls. Through the bedroom window, I had noticed a pipe that poured water all over the terrace steps whenever anyone took a bath.

"And look here," Mrs. Grail said, dashing into the laundry room. "Ah, God, it's awful." A hideous sort of vine was waving its tendrils through the cupboard door and poking out through the hinges. "That wasn't there a few days ago," I said.

"Ah, God, it's come through from the garden. The walls are full of holes."

We mopped up the water, which was very muddy indeed, and went up to the top floor to inspect the damage in Miss Pip's apartment Jordan had left some of his things there before he went to fetch us from America. Water had leaked into the closet and wet his shoes.

"Ah, God," cried Mrs. Grail, rubbing everything down with a cloth, "get your husband's things out of here; she'll come back and sell them. Look at this crazy place," she added, gesturing with her chin. "Look at the window the decorator has to measure. Special curtains for this place indeed!" The window, smaller than the others in the house, was bisected by a plywood partition dividing the room into two parts, each with half a window. The smaller part might have been intended to be a bathroom, since there was a large bathtub in it. An entry was cut into the partition, but there was no door and no toilet or sink. Miss Pip and her friend had filled the place with shabby luggage, old lamps and sagging chairs. A couple of mattresses had been thrown over the pile.

"She'll die of the cold up here under the roof," Mrs. Grail said, gesturing toward a tiny space heater in a corner. "And where's the sink? Where's the toilet? She'll have to go downstairs, and then there'll be hell to pay." Across the tiny hallway was another smaller room with one dirty window and a little unused fireplace. Except for a hair carpet pad and a child's chair with a broken rung, it was empty. "Where's the stove?" Mrs. Grail asked. "She'll have to go down for her meals, and then you'll see fireworks." She fumbled with a closet door. "It's locked," she said."Have you got a hairpin?"

"Oh, really, Mrs. Grail. I don't think we should even be here. Let's go down."

"It might be soaking in there," she responded righteously. "We need to air it. Why, the other cupboard was soaked, you know." She jerked viciously at the door and it popped open. The closet was stuffed with Mrs. Stackpole's clothes, a good many bath towels, and several sheets.

"There's your linen," Mrs. Grail said triumphantly. "Hidden up here all the time. Let's take it downstairs now."

"I can't," I said. I was dazed by the sight of the linen; I really couldn't believe it.

"You need the towels. And them twisty rags... and your bed..."

"Heaven knows we need more towels," I said, while visions of impetigo danced in my head. "And you know we're desperate for sheets. But I just can't take them. She locked them away."

Sighing and shaking her head, Mrs. Grail began to wipe off the top shelf of the closet, while I went down to answer the phone.

"Is Mrs. Stackpole there, please?"

"No, she isn't. She's in Scotland."

"Well, is Mr. Stackpole there?"

"There isn't any Mr. Stackpole," I said."I think she ate him."

There was a nervous titter. "Well, this is the electrician's wife. She called about a meter. Do you know anything about it?"

"What's a meter?"

"Well, you know, a shilling electric meter. She wanted it installed. She called several months ago, but my husband was on holiday and then he's been busy. You put a shilling in, you see, and the lights stay on for a certain time, until the shilling is used up."

I could see us all in the dark, frantically turning our pockets out, and I was very glad skilled English workmen spent most of their time on holiday.

"She won't be back until September," I said. "We've taken the house until then."

"Oh good," she said. "My husband has no time now anyway. That was what I wanted to tell her." I hung up, picturing Miss Pip hunting for shillings in the dark, and the phone rang again. This time it was Jordan. "I have to go to Birmingham next week," he said. "I just found out today. Basil Goldbrick knows about this company there that finances companies. Things are getting very bad, I don't know how long we can keep on. So Basil thinks we can do something with this company in Birmingham. He'll go up with me and introduce me to them. He knows the people or something. So Basil thinks we can do something with this company in Birmingham. He'll go up with me and introduce me to them. He knows the people or something."

It was an odd thing about Jordan's London business. It was the same kind of business he ran in Chicago, but it didn't behave at all in the same way. In London, people came to work in the morning and stayed eight hours, but since nothing seemed to get done, Jordan decided he didn't have enough people. So he kept adding people, more and more people, which cost more and more money, and still nothing got done. Whenever I went to the office I met the people, streaming through the halls on their way to the lavatory, carrying plants and handbags, or on their way to visit each other, carrying plates of cake and steaming mugs, or bringing each other sugar or extra milk. They were all very pleasant, and nodded and smiled at me. It was as though everybody were getting ready for something exciting to happen but it never happened. Bill and Jordan sat in their tiny windowless office staving off creditors; people came in all the time and brought them things to eat. Their office was littered with empty tea mugs and crocks of moldy cheese.

"That's very depressing that you have to go to Birmingham," I said. "And we have to be alone all night."

"Don't you think I'm depressed? Don't you think I find it depressing?" His voice rose.

"I suppose," I said.

There was a short pause.

"It's also depressing for the children," I said.

"Listen, why don't you call Rose Emily Foyle? I think she'll invite us out to Cramley for the afternoon on Sunday. She and Pat have two kids, you know."

"Well, if she wouldn't mind. The children need other children. Do you know her well enough to ask?"

"Of course I do. Rose Emily is very nice."

"Oh, good."

"I have to go now," Jordan said. "My tea is getting cold."

15

The Science Museum

THE NEXT DAY Jordan left for Birmingham. He wasn't coming back until the following evening. "What fun we'll have on our own," I said brightly. "We'll go to Wimpy's for dinner."

"It's spooky without Daddy," Eric said, looking around.

"It's not spooky yet," Bruce said. "It's still daylight."

The telephone rang, a fairly unusual occurrence. It was Cynthia.

"Oh, Cynthia," I said, pleased. "How good to hear from you. Jordan has just left for Birmingham and we feel sort of lonesome. Could you and Sydney come here for lunch? We could spend the afternoon together."

"I actually called to ask if you were free tomorrow night," Cynthia said.

"Well, Jordan is coming back from Birmingham fairly early…"

"Oh, good," Cynthia said. "My friend Althea wants to meet you. You'll love her. We'll drop by about seven-thirty."

"But what about today? I mean, the children would love to see Sydney and I haven't seen you for a while—"

"Oh," Cynthia said, in a feeble voice, "I have such a headache. My legs feel queer. I'm sort of sick."

"Maybe it would cheer you up to get out? Change of pace."

"I went out yesterday to a seaside restaurant," Cynthia said. "The day before that I shopped in the West End with friends. The day before that I went to a lovely tea and fashion show with other friends."

"The children would love to see Sydney," I said. "They're awfully lonely."

"Sydney has a headache," she responded promptly. "Her eyes look funny. I think she's sort of sick."

"How about tomorrow? We haven't got much to do."

"We really have to stay with my parents. You know they're getting old and I can't be here to take care of them. I have to go home soon. It's very depressing." I wondered whether the peanut eating had gotten to Cynthia. She certainly seemed changed. She had always been eager to go to lunch with me at home; of course here I didn't have a car. At any rate we arranged that she and her friend Althea would come to visit the following night.

Now we had not only an empty day ahead of us, but an empty evening as well. We decided to go to the Science Museum, which was within walking distance, across the street from the Victoria and Albert.

We had some difficulty finding the Children's Exhibits because two guides told us there weren't any, but we finally located them in the basement, in a section that was very dark, grimy and Victorian. But there were things you could work by pressing buttons and pulling levers. Bruce and Eric, happy and excited, lined up as they had always done at the Museum of Science and Industry in Chicago, and awaited their turns. There were a lot of schoolboys there, in very dirty woolen uniforms, who apparently never took turns, because they stayed endlessly at the machines. A few times Bruce and Eric got through: while they were turning knobs and looking through holes, boys came up and casually knocked them out of the way. "Hey!" I kept saying indignantly. "Stop that!" They didn't pay any attention to me. Some of the scuffling among the schoolboys themselves got very rough indeed. There didn't seem to be any supervision.

We went upstairs for tea. The top floors of the Museum were new, beautiful and airy, and devoted to ships and airplanes. The cafeteria offered a good view of the city. The tables were sticky and so were the trays; I noticed that the attendants took the trays off the tables and put them back on the racks to be used again without washing them. But the sandwiches, which were wrapped in waxed paper, were tasty and the Coca Cola was cold. We liked the cafeteria.

After tea, we admired the airplane exhibits: you could go up a sort of catwalk and look closely at the early planes, which hung from the ceiling. Then we descended to the Children's Exhibits again; a good many of the kiddies had been collected and taken away, so it was possible to walk about without being knocked down. We stayed there a long time, and then went out and wandered about Knightsbridge, looking at the shops.

It was finally dinnertime, and Mark met us at Wimpy's, as we had arranged. He looked morose.

"I don't like the office so much anymore," he said.

"What happened?" I asked, surprised. "You loved it."

"I'll go," Bruce said.

"I'll go," Eric said.

"They keep laughing at my shoes," Mark said.

"What's wrong with your shoes?" I said. "I like your shoes."

"They've got laces. The toes aren't pointed."

"You've got flat feet."

"They don't like my jacket either," he said.

"My God, is it an office or Christian Dior?"

"Jane keeps calling me a twit," Mark said.

"She called *me* an old cow," I said. "Your father says it's just her way." She had recently handed me some kind of liquid medicine for a headache, and when I said I would prefer aspirin, she had given me a friendly shove and said, "Go on, you old cow, drink it." "She's very informal," I added, through gritted teeth.

"Today she called me a fathead," Mark said.

"She expects everyone to love her," I remarked.

"*I* love her," Eric said.

"The others laugh at me too," Mark said. "They say awful things about America."

I tried to think of something positive to say. In the newspapers and on television, in book reviews, television reviews, film reviews, editorials; on panel shows, in musical reviews, in dramas, one encountered an unmistakable hostility toward Americans. To be fair, foreigners in general were derided. But one sensed an obsession with America.

"They say our shoes are ugly and our clothes are ugly," Mark said mournfully.

"They should talk," I said, deteriorating into a rage that surprised me, "with those crazy clodhoppers of theirs."

"I feel sorry for them," Mark said, suddenly switching attitudes and leaving me with my hostilities hanging out, as usual. "Today Jane was wearing this terrible dress, like cardboard, with holes in the sleeves. I mean it had holey sleeves. She just bought it, and she was so proud of it. It made me feel sad."

"I suppose she *could* be pretty," I said.

"She's beautiful," Eric said.

"I feel sorry for all of them," Mark said. "They're so poor and miserable."

"Then don't complain," I snapped.

"I like it here," Mark said. "You're ruining it for me. You hate it. I can tell."

"I don't hate it," I said. "All my life I've loved England. I'm an English major, aren't I?"

Eric began to cry. "I'm afraid of Hamlet's uncle," he said. "I'm afraid of King Claudius. I want to go home."

16
At the Pub

THE CHILDREN WERE SETTLED in front of the TV set watching some terrible programs the next evening, when Cynthia arrived with her friend Althea Bradgood. Althea was in her early forties, wearing a pre-war hairdo, no makeup and no-nonsense clothes. In order not to disturb the children, I suggested we go upstairs to the master bedroom, which had a stiff little eighteenth-century sofa. Cynthia had brought me some mints.

"I'm afraid Jordan isn't back yet," I said, shoveling several pounds of clean laundry off the sofa onto the floor.

"This place is just like home, isn't it?" Cynthia said, eyeing the mess.

"I'm afraid Jordan hasn't returned from Birmingham yet," I said to Althea.

"Birmingham!" Cynthia cried. "Why would anyone want to go to Birmingham? It's terribly vulgar."

"Don't tell me," Althea said to me. "Let me guess. You're a Pisces."

"Althea is very interested in astrology," Cynthia said.

"Oh, Pisces," I said. "No, actually. Jordan is a Pisces. I'm a Virgo."

"You can't be," Althea said.

I insisted I was.

"But you can't be. You walk like a Pisces. You gesture like a Pisces. Your whole personality is Pisces." She thought about it. "Two stars must have crossed. Something is wrong. You're a Pisces. I never make a mistake."

"Have a mint," I said.

"Oh, you're very kind," Althea said, taking one.

"What have *you* been doing?" Cynthia asked me. "We went to the beach for two days. It was a lovely house, very lush. And last evening we went to a place called Crockford's. Percival Epstein took us. It was very impressive. I believe many titled people go there. I saw many women with jewels all over them. Percival gave me twenty pounds and I gambled with it."

"Did you win?"

She smiled. "It's a very exclusive place, Crockford's," she said. "We had a delicious dinner. For lunch I went to a charming little place in Soho. My friends have been simply wonderful. They're so loyal."

"You'll be sorry to leave," I said.

"There's nothing like getting home," Cynthia said severely. "I'm always glad to get home."

"That gesture you just made was pure Pisces," Althea said to me.

"Oh, here's Jordan now," I said, peering out the window. "He just got out of a cab."

Joyous noises drifted up the stairs, followed by Jordan, looking tired.

"I loved Birmingham," he said, after greeting me and Cynthia, and being introduced to Althea. "It's very alive. I mean there's a real feeling of activity there, commercial activity. They're rebuilding some of it. It's very exciting."

"I'm happy to say that I've never been to Birmingham," Cynthia said merrily.

"Is your wife really Virgo?" Althea asked Jordan. "I feel she's Pisces."

"*I'm* Pisces," Jordan said.

"Why don't we all go over to the pub?" I said. "You must be hungry, Jordan. I'm afraid there's nothing to eat here."

"There's nothing to eat here?" Cynthia asked.

"I'm afraid not," I said. "I sort of planned on going to the pub."

"Oh, that's a good idea," Jordan said. "I'll have a sandwich there."

"It's only across the street," I said to Cynthia, who looked rather downcast.

In the cozy pub, just on the corner of Baldridge Place across the street from Number Sixteen, a fat man, surrounded by admirers, was saying loudly, "... and we had this delightful little mews flat. But when we came home from the theater one evening, there they all were, outside in deck chairs. Well, one needs to be rather frigid with people like that, doesn't one?"

We slipped into chairs; several dogs looked at us suspiciously. "What a charming place," Cynthia said. "I'd like a Scotch and soda. I'm not hungry."

"I'll have a gin anything," I said, looking at the fat man and his admirers. "I'm not hungry either."

"Just pineapple juice for me," Althea said. "You're so kind."

"Nothing alcoholic?"

"Oh, dear, I don't drink."

Jordan went to the bar to get the drinks.

"You used to drink," Cynthia said to Althea.

"Oh, I used to drink a great deal," Althea said. "I drank and drank. But it wasn't right and I knew it wasn't right. Not just for religious reasons, although religious reasons count. But I gave it up at the same time that I gave up meat. We all drink too much," Althea said to me. "British people drink too much."

Cynthia stirred indignantly.

"I became disgusted," Althea went on. "Seeing people being sick on the underground on Saturday night."

"Who?" Cynthia asked.

"Lots of people. Many British people. I saw them being sick on the underground on Saturday night; it was most upsetting. I was sick myself; not on the underground of course. I waited until I got home."

"I never saw anyone being sick on the underground," Cynthia said.

"Oh, I did. Many times," Althea responded firmly.

"I never heard anyone else say it," Cynthia said.

"It's one of the things which decided me to give up drink," Althea replied.

Jordan returned with a tray of glasses and a sandwich for himself.

"What a pleasant place," Cynthia said, looking around.

"It is pleasant," I said, looking at the fat man. "But an awful lot of phonies come in here."

"I don't see any," Cynthia said.

"What delicious pineapple juice," Althea remarked.

"I saw the most charming thing today," Cynthia said. "A woman was pushing a pram down the street with a little boy in it. I heard her say, 'You've been naughty. Now you can't have a sweetie.'" She chuckled. "Isn't that darling? 'A sweetie.' In

America," she went on, her voice dropping, "in America he'd have been given a huge sack of sweets just to *be* naughty."

"I can't remember when I've tasted such delicious pineapple juice," Althea said.

"Why don't you move back here, Cynthia?" I asked, when I was able to talk.

"I should like very much to do that," Cynthia said. "But it would have to be under the best possible circumstances. Financially," She sipped delicately at her drink. "I should certainly," she went on comfortably, "be happier back here, where people are civilized and know how to behave properly. Everywhere I go here I'm pushed and shoved by American tourists."

"It has a lovely flavor," Althea said. "The juice."

"Aren't you an American?" Jordan said to Cynthia.

She laughed. "Of course not. I'm English."

"But you became an American citizen."

"Oh, yes, I became an American citizen, but I'm English."

"But you took an oath to uphold America, to defend it, to defend American institutions. They made you a citizen. That makes you an American."

Cynthia thought it over.

"I suppose I *am* an American citizen," she said. "But I'm English."

"Would you like another pineapple juice?" Jordan asked Althea.

"Oh, you're so kind," Althea said. "Oh, aren't you kind. I don't want another one, because it does queer things to my digestion, but I think you're awfully kind. Thank you so much, but I really don't want another one. I loved it, it was delicious, but I don't feel that I want another one. But you are kind."

She took a small book and pencil from her bag. "I should like to take you and the boys to Derry & Toms," she said. "It has a famous roof garden. I should like to take you there on a Saturday morning."

"Oh, Derry's is beautiful," Cynthia cried. "It's ever so much nicer than Marshall Field's. It has a famous roof garden, growing miles above the city." Althea named a day in July and wrote it down. "I'm going away; I shall be back then. I know it seems distant, but these things are on you before you know it."

"We have to go," Cynthia said. "We'll miss the last bus."

"You've got bags of time," Jordan said, employing an Anglicism.

"I can't bear the prospect of missing the bus," Cynthia said, rising.

We walked to the bus stop through the chilly evening.

"The children would love to see Sydney," I said, knowing it was hopeless. "They're awfully lonely."

"Oh, I'll keep in touch with you," Cynthia said. The big red bus came into view. We said a warm goodbye to Althea. "You know my parents are getting older," Cynthia called, getting on the bus. "I can't be here to look after them. It's awfully sad. Goodbye, thanks for the drinks."

17

At Rose Emily's

ON SUNDAY we were set to visit with Pat Foyle's family in Cramley. "The children can play with other children," Jordan said. "That's what they need. And you'll enjoy getting out of London. It's nice in Cramley."

We had been invited to come for tea, so we left about one o'clock. It wasn't raining or cloudy as it had been all week; pale Sunday sunlight streamed about us. We left from Marylebone Station; it was old and airy, rather like a Victorian birdcage. I liked it, in a pale Victorian sort of way.

A man and a woman and some teenagers were in the coach with us. Halfway there they began to giggle loudly and play hide and seek behind the seats. Once in a while one of them fell down. Sometimes it was the woman, who looked to be in her fifties.

"I suppose Pat will be there," I said. "He wouldn't be working on Sunday."

"Well, he might be," Jordan said. "Of course with this situation the chances are he won't."

"What situation?"

"Oh, didn't I tell you? I thought I told you. He's living with some other woman in a neighboring town. It's been going on for a couple of weeks. Rose Emily is awfully upset."

"What are we going there for?" I said, agitated. "How can we inflict ourselves on her at a time like this?"

"What do you mean?" Jordan said. "She's fine."

Rose Emily was waiting at the station, a tall handsome woman in a wrinkled skirt and bare legs. "We'll have to walk home," she said. "Pat's got the car, of course." Two children were with her. "This is Judith and this is Charles," she said. Judith was about ten and had long black hair and piercing eyes. Charles, about Eric's age, was small and wiry; he peered at us through a heavy thatch of hair. "Run along," Rose Emily said to the children.

She grasped Jordan's arm and drew him ahead, talking to him animatedly. Some of her sentences drifted back to Mark, Bruce and me on the quiet air. "Simply don't *understand*..." she said, and "... told him repeatedly..." We climbed through hedges and across fields. Weeds waved about our knees. "They're trying to put council housing in this field," Rose Emily called back to me. "We're fighting it tooth and nail. Wreck the field and the dreadful people.... Dropped in this morning and took them for ice cream," she said to Jordan.

All the houses in Cramley were built of the same brownish brick; they had small-paned windows and a weathered look, although they seemed to be relatively new. Rose Emily's house had a large garden with flower beds and vines. The living room had sliding doors opening onto the garden, and a little 1930ish *moderne* fireplace with a painting of cows hanging over it. There was a sagging sofa covered with a vaguely Spanish throw.

"I'll show you the kitchen," Rose Emily said, "and we'll carry the tea things out. We'll be much nicer outside today."

The kitchen was extremely small, and festooned with washing. We fought our way through damp sheets and towels and emerged with trays of chipped crockery. I had brought a cake.

"Perhaps you don't like tea?" Rose Emily said to me. "Many Americans don't. Would you like milk or lime juice?"

Tortured by thirst, I chose lime juice, forgetting that it would come from a bottle straight from the warm cupboard. Sweet and sticky, it clung to my dry throat as it went down. We all crouched around a low table. The air was very damp and warm, and quiet. Very quiet.

"I just love cake," Judith said, staring at me with her piercing black eyes. "I love most things. I love to eat. Mummy says I have a wonderful appetite. Don't I, Mummy?"

"Yes, you do, dear," her mother said.

"There's almost nothing I don't like to eat," Judith said. "I love everything. Charles is picky. Isn't he, Mummy?"

"Yes, he is, dear."

"Let's go play," Charles said to Eric. His accent was distinctly different from his mother's and sister's.

"Yes, go play," Rose Emily said dreamily. "But mind the flowers. Mind the bushes. Mind the currants."

"Perhaps they oughtn't to play," I said. "They might step on something."

"Oh, ducky," Rose Emily said, "don't fuss so. Not to worry. They're fine."

"It's lovely for us to get out of the city," I said. "The children have nowhere to play there."

"I used to dislike tomatoes," Judith said. "But I like them now. Mummy and I could never decide why I disliked tomatoes. We thought perhaps it was because of the pips."

"I disliked tomatoes when I was a child," Rose Emily said. "But I'm not sure now why."

"I think it was the pips, Mummy," Judith said.

"Yes, perhaps it was because of the pips. Charles! Mind the currants! Mind the blackberries!"

"I'm sure it's the pips," Judith said. "They get in your teeth and slide all over your tongue. It's horrible having tomato pips in your teeth. Look, Mummy, they're stepping on those vines." She stood up; her face turned crimson.

"Get out of those vines, you horrid, horrid boys!" she shrieked.

Eric stood still and stared at us, startled. Charles seized the opportunity to dump a bucket of grass clippings over his head.

"Stop that, Charles, you fool," Rose Emily said mildly. "He picks up disgusting habits," she said to us, "from his hideous little pals at the state school." She smiled brightly at me. "Jordan tells me you just got your degree."

"Yes," I said, "in English literature."

"Milton lived near here," she said. "He wrote most of *Paradise Lost* near here. His house is just over the way."

"My goodness, "I said. "I'd love to see it."

"Oh, it's so exciting that you got your degree," Rose Emily said. "It's marveys really. Did you write a thesis?"

"No, I took an exam. From Chaucer to the present...."

"Oh, Chaucer!" Rose Emily said. "I've always wanted to read Chaucer, but they wouldn't let us read it unexpurgated at school. They didn't let you read it all, did they?"

"Well, yes," I murmured. "Graduate school..."

"Really? They let women? Charles! Mind the bushes! Charles!"

"Oh, look what they're doing, Mummy," Judith said. She leaped to her feet. "They're stepping all over the flowers. They're naughty, horrid boys!"

She rushed at Charles, who ducked lithely away.

"Oh, children," Rose Emily said, giving me a big smile. "I really am awfully glad to meet you at last," she said. "We're all so fond of Jordan." She gave him a big smile too. "We just think Jordan's so much fun. We really enjoy him."

I murmured gratitude.

"He's not the least bit American," Rose Emily said.

"Do you mean," I said, trying to make a joke, "he's un-American?"

"I mean he's not American. You know. One meets Americans, one really feels pushed to the wall. They push, you know." She gave all of us a big smile. "But Jordan's different. He's not pushy." At this point Bruce, who had been sitting next to me in a frozen stupor similar to Mark's, rose uncertainly to his feet. His face was beet red and his cheeks were swollen; his eyes were filled with tears, and in an agony of shyness and outrage, he kept them on the ground. "Lots of English people are pushy too," he said, in a strangled voice.

"Oh, yeah," Rose Emily said.

"Bruce," I said weakly, "we don't speak… We…"

Jordan put his arm around Bruce, and Judith, from the bottom of the garden, gave a piercing scream. We all turned; she was writhing on the ground, crying and screaming and clutching her leg.

Rose Emily flew to her. "My baby!" she cried, "What is it?"

"Charles," Judith shrieked, "Charles."

"What has he done, Judith?"

Charles appeared to have climbed a tree. Rose Emily half carried Judith to the tea table.

"Oh, that dreadful wretch Charles," Judith said. "It's his fault."

"Oh, Charles," Rose Emily cried, "what have you done?"

"I kicked his bicycle and hurt my leg," Judith sobbed. "It's all his fault."

Mark made a sort of choking sound.

"Oh, Charles, do be careful," Rose Emily said.

Charles climbed down from the tree, and began to pry up the sewer lid that was under our feet.

"Look," he said, in a rich Cockney, "'ere's the sewer, I'll show you." It was the sewer all right.

"I think," Jordan said, "if we're going to get the six o'clock train, we really ought to help you clear away now. We can have a leisurely walk to the station. We don't mind waiting there."

"No, that's right," I said. "I mean I hate to rush."

"Yeah," Mark said, his first word of the afternoon.

We fought our way through the wet laundry again and deposited the crockery.

"You must take your cake back with you," Rose Emily said to me. "There's some left."

"No, that's for you," I said grandly.

"Oh, thanks awfully," Rose Emily said. "It's super cake."

"You're not all that tall when you stand up," Judith said, staring at me. "You're short."

"Charles!" Rose Emily shouted, "Put down that sewer lid! Look out for the bushes! Julia goes to France in August," she said to me, "and then perhaps I'll ring you. I may come in town with Charles."

"Oh, that would be nice," I said. Eric was standing next to me, trying to scratch the grass clippings out of his collar.

We began our trek back across the fields and over the hedges. Charles climbed trees and jumped over walls and threw pebbles at Eric, who was sucking his thumb. Rose Emily walked on ahead with Jordan and snatches of her conversation floated back to us. "Taking my money," she said, "and not a cent… Definitely starting proceedings, and yet I feel…."

Mark walked beside me, his arm protectively around Bruce. "Oh, boy," he said softly.

18

Day Camp

We rose very early on Monday, our first day at day camp. Jordan took us in a cab to the South Kensington—he and Mark kept calling it South Ken—underground station. He made inquiries, handed me a little colored map and he and Mark rushed off. The children and I waited on a platform with several large bearded men in turbans who looked like extras in an old Ronald Colman movie, and a knobby Buddhist priest carrying prayer beads. It was a long ride to West Ruyslip, but we all felt cheerful because at least we were going somewhere and not just wandering around looking for happiness.

West Ruyslip was the end of the line. We disembarked, surprised to smell trees and flowers, and walked half a block down a hill to the American Air Force base. There large people in uniforms blocked our way, looking at us suspiciously. Some of them wanted us to go away, but I stood my ground and finally an officer told them that the day camp was open to civilians, and it was all right. A uniformed person took us across the camp to a wooden building. The ground was brown and bare; it had started to rain, and an icy wind was blowing.

I signed the boys into the camp for one week and hung around in a large auditorium while the lady from Texas sorted all the children into groups. Bruce and Eric were in the same group. She gave them all paper Indian headdresses and told them to run around in a circle. At this point I went out into the hall because I could feel Bruce trying to catch my eye. I sat down on a bench in the hall and started to read. The rain beat on the tin roof of the building and the winds swirled about it. I was reading a British reprint of an American novel about a sensitive man who lived in New Jersey and felt stifled. His wife joined the PTA and he was booed at meetings.

I visited the lavatory and was shocked to find lewd things written all over the walls; severe notes from the authorities were posted threatening to shut the ladies off from a lavatory entirely if they did not mend their ways. Finally, suffering from cold, headache and general malaise, I went to the base cafeteria for lunch, to find that they would not take my English money. A young American girl gave me some American change, and we sat together to eat.

"I've been here three years," she said. "I hate it. They call us Yanks, we call them Blokes. The children beat up my little sister. I have to stay here because I'm getting married and my fiancé hasn't finished here. Everybody makes fun of my accent. I do telephone ordering for the base; yesterday a man said he couldn't understand a word I said. He said he didn't know what language I was speaking."

She went off moodily and I went back to my draughty hallway and my book. After an hour or so I wandered into the office to thaw out. The girls there were chatting. "I'm getting out," one said. "I'm going to college in the States. I feel awfully sorry for my mother, though; she's got another year here. She wants to come with me and settle me in college, but my father won't let her because he's afraid she won't come back."

"I just got back from Manchester," another one said. "We had a ball."

"You liked Manchester?" I said.

"Oh, it was great. The people are friendly up there. Not like London. They're almost like Americans up there."

I huddled in the office until four o'clock when I collected Eric, who said he had had a good time, and Bruce, who was too miserable even to complain, and we walked back to the underground where we changed trains once, traveling on a monumental escalator, and then reached South Ken where we took a cab home. The house was dark and very cold. Eric went into the little lavatory on the ground floor.

"Hey, it's all wet back there," he said.

I went back. Water was running down the wall between the lavatory and the small study.

"Oh, dear," I said, "I'll call Mr. MacAllister."

"… and there's quite a lot of water coming down the wall," I said to him on the phone.

For some incomprehensible reason, Mr. MacAllister laughed.

"How awful for you," he said.

"Yes," I said. "Well, do you know a plumber?"

Mr. MacAllister's voice became rather frigid. "I don't *know* any plumbers," he said. "I do know *of* a builder."

"Well, do you think you could call him? Someone is here every day until two o'clock."

"Well, I could try to call him, yes."

"Because you see," I said slowly and distinctly, "there's quite a lot of water coming down the wall."

Mr. MacAllister laughed, and we rang off.

19

Shopping

THE NEXT MORNING I phoned the day camp, as I had been instructed to do, to find out what their field trip plans were, and whether, if they were coming to London, we could meet them somewhere. Bruce was barely speaking to me, because he had spent his entire day running around in circles wearing a paper hat. Eric had been more vocal on the subject. "No, I didn't like it," he said, "but at least it was something to do."

The people at the day camp informed me that they were going to be at Madame Tussaud's in an hour. This was not good news. Eric was still afraid of Hamlet's uncle. He wouldn't go upstairs alone and every time we went out, he asked whether we were going near Madame Tussaud's.

Now I had to announce that the day camp was going there.

"I want to go to Madame Tussaud's again," Bruce said instantly.

"So do I," Eric said. He looked doubtful.

"But it frightened you," I said.

"I want to go," Bruce said. "Eric doesn't have to go, but I want to."

"I want to, too," Eric said. He still looked doubtful.

I began to rationalize. "Maybe," I said, "maybe if you go again, you'll see how you built the whole thing up in your mind, and you'll realize how silly it is to be frightened. Do you think so?"

"Yes," Eric said.

"I mean," I went on, gaining confidence, "that was the only time you went, and we had just arrived, and everything seemed so strange to you. But if you go again, with a lot of other children, you'll see it in a different sort of light."

"Yes, I will," Eric said.

"No, he won't," Bruce said. "He'll be scared out of his wits."

"Maybe he won't, Bruce," I said. "Why don't we give it a try?"

"There's a lot of water coming down the wall of the lavatory," Mrs. Grail said, coming into the room. "The carpet's getting soaked." I told her that I had called Mr. MacAllister.

"I think someone will come in today and fix it."

"Ah, that awful thing," Mrs. Grail said automatically.

"Yes, but he knows *of* a builder," I said. "He doesn't *know* any plumbers."

"Ah, the snobs," Mrs. Grail said.

Half an hour later we found the Air Force children bunched up in a disorganized un-English way in front of Madame Tussaud's. The distracted Texas lady was waiting for us.

"I couldn't decide whether Eric should go," I said, "but we all decided it would take the curse off it for him if he went again, especially with a lot of other children."

"Why, it surely would," the Texas lady said.

"I mean," I said, "we are assuming that he was frightened the first time only because it was a strange sort of day and we were all three alone here. We think that with a lot of children he will feel different, and anyway—"

"Why, surely," the lady said, counting heads. "Don't worry about a thing."

She herded them away while I was still saying, "It's possible that...."

Eric waved gaily to me as he went in.

I was free at last.

* * *

I could go shopping. I could wander around looking in shop windows. I knew already that everything was expensive. I returned to Knightsbridge and stopped at a shoe store. There were black patent leather sandals in the window. The very thing. The man who greeted me at the door was friendly to the point of being obsequious; he handed me and the shoe in question to a young saleslady, or shop assistant, who eyed me with distaste.

"Yes?" she said.

I told her that I wanted the shoe in question in my size.

"I don't know what sizes we have left," she said.

"Perhaps you could measure my foot," I said, adding apologetically, "If I could sit down...."

She hesitated and then led me down some stairs to another shoe salon. She measured my foot, vanished, and reappeared with a rather large sandal, which she placed on my foot and then whisked off, just as I was about to stand.

"It doesn't fit you," she said. "We don't have it in your size."

"Do you have anything else that would fit me?"

"Not an open shoe like that," she said, and rose briskly.

"How about a closed one?" I asked.

She went away, looking annoyed, and came back almost immediately to say firmly, "We don't have anything for you in black." Unwilling to annoy her further by requesting a color, I went out into the street again, and decided to buy some glasses for an evening party that Jordan wanted to give. There was an enormous crush in the shop. I ruined a young man's day by asking him if he were free, or if he could get me a salesperson. He was wearing a suit so I thought he was a manager. His hand flew to his throat. "I'm not..." he murmured, "shop... assistant...."

"Oh, I'm sorry. I thought you were—"

"I hope," he breathed, "I don't look like one...."

"No, no," I said. "It's just that I'm confused. I don't know what I'm doing."

This seemed to offer him solace, and on that note I pushed off, deciding to forget the glasses and go to Jordan's office, where, I had heard, all sorts of subtle class distinctions and various hostilities had cropped up. Mark had mentioned that some people were behaving badly toward Vincent and other employees of color. Obviously I couldn't do anything about that, but I thought I might be able to cheer Jordan up. Anyway, I didn't have anywhere else to go.

Harried streams of ladies in lumpy cardigans pushed pleasantly past me in the narrow corridor. Jordan and Bill Dworkin were crouched glumly in their tiny office. A faint odor of mold pervaded everything. Mark was busy reproducing Beatle photographs on the copy machine.

"How are things?" I asked, without much hope
A faint sigh stirred the dampness.

"It's like a swamp in here," I said. Jordan muttered something.

At this point Eric and Bruce entered.

"What are you doing here?" I said, startled. "It's not even two o'clock."

"He got scared," Bruce said. "He got scared all over again at Madame Tussaud's and we had to leave. I wasn't scared, I was enjoying it, but I had to leave because of him."

"I got scared," Eric said, smiling self-consciously.

"So we took a cab," Bruce continued. "We took a cab over here and I had enough money, and a shilling tip. And Eric left his raincoat and his sweater in the cab."

"His new raincoat," I said. "His new sweater."

"I noticed it right away," Bruce said. "I called the man, but he just drove off."

"What kind of idiot just drives off without checking the back seat after little children?" I demanded indignantly of Jordan. He gave another weary sigh and waved his hand weakly. "You'd better take them away," he said. "Things are fouled up enough around here as it is."

"Come on, boys," I said, with my big false grin. "Let's go to Selfridge's and have a nice drink or something. They have tasty scones at Selfridge's," I said to Jordan in an aside. I had had tea there once with Marilyn, an American friend. Her husband was doing research at the British Museum and she consequently spent a lot of time in London, studying Yoga and flower arranging and hanging around. I had asked her how she liked being there. She said she did and she didn't. She found housekeeping difficult and she didn't like shopping. She and her husband ate a lot of cabbages.

I confessed that I was afraid to go into a butcher shop.

Marilyn said that she had always been afraid to go into butcher shops in London. "But you have to be firm with them," she said, "you can't let them bully you." A week earlier, her husband had said he was sick of eating cabbage. When they went out for an evening walk, he had pointed out a roast in a butcher's window and told her to go in the next day and buy it for dinner. "So," she said, "the next morning I went in there and there was this butcher." She put on a face of eighteenth-century hauteur, and lounged languidly behind an imaginary counter.

"So I said, 'You know that roast in the window?' And he said..." She drew herself up, her face froze, and her voice dripped icicles. 'That is a... stuffed... rolled lamb, Madam.' So I said to him, 'Well, there's a fly on it.' And I left. You have to be firm with them."

"So," I said, "you didn't actually buy the meat."

"Well, no. We had cabbage for dinner. But it's all a question of handling them. For instance, I buy this cheese at a market. They sell it in this big block, and I have to slice it. So I asked them to slice it. I said, 'Could you slice it?' and they always said, 'Oh, no, Madam, we couldn't possibly slice it.' So I thought about it, and the next time I said, 'You couldn't possibly slice it,' and the man said, 'Oh, yes, of course we can, Madam.' You have to know how to handle them."

All in all, it had been an entertaining tea, and the scones were delicious, so I decided to take the boys to Selfridge's. "You couldn't come, could you, Mark?" I asked wistfully.

"Yes, I could," he said promptly.

"We need you here," his father said lugubriously.

"I'll be back tomorrow," Mark said.

"The poor little tyke is all yellow," I said. "He needs fresh air." Actually, we were all a bit yellow, because the sun rarely shone and the air was permanently soggy.

The ladies were coming around with their cracked cups and slices of cake, as they seemed to do every hour in that office. We left Jordan moodily drinking his brown tea, while Bill entertained him with a story about two more rude Americans who had pushed in front of him in the post office.

20

Chocolate and the Zoo

"YOUR FATHER'S VERY NERVOUS," I said to Mark.

"That place gets on your nerves," he said. "Tomorrow I'm going to Carnaby Street to buy some clothes"

"What's that?"

"Carnaby Street. It's where all the Mods buy their clothes. They have cool clothes. The Beatles' tailor is there, the Stones shop there. This is a very cool place," he said contentiously. "The music is great. You don't appreciate it."

"I do appreciate it," I said, stung. "All my life I've loved England."

We took a cab to Selfridge's and fought our way through the crowds to the Jungle Room on an upper floor. "It doesn't look like much," I said apologetically, "but the scones are good."

"I want some ice cream," Mark said.

"They have ice cream."

We sat down next to the wall; there were large jungly-looking leaves on the wallpaper.

"Boy, is this creepy-looking," Mark said. When the waitress came to our table, Bruce and I ordered scones. Eric said he wanted chocolate milk. He was always demanding outrageous things: chocolate milk, coke without lemon, more toast, no prawns.... Now at Selfridge's, I was telling the waitress, "He'll have chocolate milk."

"Oh, we don't do chocolate milk," she replied. She was a pretty girl, with a fresh complexion. "We *do* do chocolate sodas," she added, kindly.

"Well," I said, "if you make... if you do chocolate sodas, you must have chocolate syrup."

"Y e-e-s," she said doubtfully.

"And if you have milk, all you have to do is take a few spoonsful of chocolate syrup and put it in the milk and stir it up, and you've got chocolate milk."

There was a pause.

"What?" she said.

"You see," I said, "you have the chocolate syrup in a jar or something. You pour a glass of milk. Then you take a spoon and you put syrup on the spoon and put the spoon into the milk and stir it up and you have chocolate milk."

"You mean," she said, "that you mix...? You put...?"

"Yes, you put the chocolate syrup on a spoon, into the glass of milk, a few times, and you mix it or stir it, and that makes chocolate milk." I didn't look at the children while this conversation was taking place.

"I'll go and check," the waitress said. "See if it can be done."

She went off, and after a while she came back with a dramatic announcement. "We can do it!" she cried triumphantly.

"It's all in handling them," I said smugly.

"I don't believe this," Mark said.

She brought the scones, some tea, a chocolate soda for Mark, a glass of milk for Bruce and a glass of heavily chocolate milk for Eric.

"The soda looks good," I said to Mark. It was tall and topped with whipped cream and a cherry.

He took a deep swig through the straw and his face turned purple. "It's all hot chocolate on the bottom," he said, when he could talk. "Only the chocolate came through, and they *heated* it."

I said they couldn't possibly have heated it. "Well, it's awfully warm. Visualize this: you take a deep drink, you're thirsty. You expect a cool swig of ice cream. You get hot syrup. Faugh."

"Mix it up," I said. "You take a spoon and you put it in, and you move it—"

"There's too much chocolate in this milk," Eric said. "I can't drink it."

"You have to drink it," Bruce said. "Look what she went through."

"Pour it in your shoe," Mark said. "She won't know." We went home, to find the wall streaked and peeling, and the carpet black and soggy.

"The plumber didn't come," I said. "I'd better call him myself."

I studied Mrs. Stackpole's lists and came up with a telephone number.

"Is Mr. Kradge there?"

"No, I'm afraid he's away."

"Oh. Well, this is Mrs. Miller. I'm renting Mrs. Stackpole's house for the summer, and she left Mr. Kradge's name...."

"Mr. Kradge is on holiday."

"When do you expect him back? Or could you send someone else? You see, there's a lot of water...."

"When he comes in," she said, losing her patience, "I'll send him round."

"But when do you expect him? I think it's an emergency."

"He's on holiday. When he comes back," she said, evidently through clenched teeth, "I'll... send... him... round." There wasn't any business section in the phone book, so we were dependent on Mr. Kradge.

The next day the Air Force camp was going to the zoo. We had already been to the zoo on a Sunday, but we decided to go again because there was nothing else to do and the Air Force children cheered us up. They were a pleasant lot, friendly and agreeable. The London Zoo was a very good zoo and we roamed around, enjoying it. It was a sunny day. Eric found a stand that sold cold milk, and he kept buying and drinking it.

"It's really cold," he said, surprised.

The elephants were interesting: they stood near a railing and ate what people gave them. All the children gave them peanuts. Eric gave his elephant all the peanuts he had. "Now give them the bag," a little boy said to Eric. Before I could stop him, Eric, impressionable as always, put the little empty peanut bag in the elephant's trunk.

"Oh, Eric," I said, reaching toward him, "that wasn't... you really shouldn't..."

Before I could go on, I was shoved rather roughly aside, and a man in his fifties with a brown moustache and popping eyes had seized Eric's arm. "You mustn't do that," the man gasped, shaking all over. "You mustn't tease animals. If you... if you tease animals, they'll be angry with you, and... and... hit you!"

"The elephant spit it out, mister," one of the children said soothingly.

The man released Eric's arm and trembled off, on the verge of tears.

"I want to go home," Eric said.

I noticed a violent reaction in myself. Crazy English animal lover, I thought.

At this point the chimpanzees provided a distraction. One of them grabbed a pocket handkerchief and pretended to cry into it, and the other one came up to the bars and spat at the crowd which screamed and ducked. I was fascinated with this spectacle and when I finally turned away, I discovered that we had lost the Air Force camp. We wandered around for a while looking for them and buying cold milk; finally I got a map and tried to find the exit. I am very bad at reading maps and soon we found ourselves in the wilds of Regent's Park. It was incredibly large and empty. We walked and walked, sitting on benches periodically to recoup our strength. Eventually, we stumbled on a place that sold cold bottled drinks and near that a large pond with boats for rent. At last we had found something both children enjoyed.

I sat on a bench and Bruce and Eric swirled round and round the pond in motor boats. I read a paperback, looking up occasionally to watch the boat boys, in rubber hip boots, disentangle boats and give people starts. These boys were thin and rather undersized; they were surly with the customers and nasty to each other. A very elegant lady came up, holding a little girl by the hand. An obvious nanny was with her, pushing a boy about a year old in a stroller. The nanny went off in a boat with the little girl, and the elegant lady sat down beside me, arranging the baby, who had a fat face and was wearing a small blue overcoat with brass buttons. He bounced up and down and pointed to the water.

"Oh, Oliver," the lady said. "Do sit still. Don't squirm so."

"Wah, wah!" Oliver said. "Blah. Wah. Goo goo."

"Oh, Oliver," the lady said, with distaste. "Do be sensible."

21

Evening at Maud Tweak's

WE CAME HOME FROM THE PARK in a cheerful mood for a change, ignoring the peeling wall and the soaked carpet. Jordan and I were going out that evening. A woman named Maud Tweak had invited us to dinner. She was in public relations; that was how Jordan had met her: she used his newspaper clipping service. She had phoned me the week before to set up a date between Eric and a little boy named Michael, the son of Margaret, a friend of hers. We were supposed to meet Michael and Margaret on a Saturday afternoon to see a film called *Dr. Who and the Daleks,* which was all the rage in London. We were to meet in the theater lobby; Margaret would be wearing a white carnation or something, and holding little Michael by the hand. I said "Fine," and Maud and Margaret said "Jolly good," and it was arranged.

We had arrived to find a line, or queue, extending from the box office all the way around the side of the theater into a small alley, or mews. We had to wait almost an hour in the alley, but it wasn't boring. A group of itinerant musicians called The Happy Warriors traveled up and down the queue, playing music. They were all old and shabby and their music was terrible. A very old man with watery eyes moved in front of them, holding out a ragged cap, his ancient overcoat dragging in the gutter. They were a London institution. Bruce took one look at them and turned a pale shade of green.

"They're *beggars,*" he whispered, and dumped all his money into the filthy cap.

"Some people think they're charming," I said to Bruce.

"Charming!" he said.

"I want to know the difference between a movie and a show," Eric said suddenly.

"Well, it depends what you mean," I said. "Some people call a movie a show. When I was little, I called a movie a show."

"But what's the difference?" Eric asked.

"Sometimes there isn't any. But a show can be—"

"A show is on a stage and a movie is a movie," the woman behind us said impatiently. She turned to her children and said loudly, "This little boy is being silly and asking stupid questions."

I had noticed and was to notice a free and easy attitude toward other people's children in London.

We finally got into *Dr. Who and the Daleks,* which we enjoyed. We were surprised to see people sitting and standing in the aisles, but none of them appeared to be wearing white carnations, and we went home without meeting Margaret and Michael. Now we were going to meet Margaret, because she and her friend Albert were picking us up in a minicab to take us to Maud Tweak's. We kissed the children goodnight, and went off happily.

"I hope you don't mind garlic," Albert said as we climbed into the minicab. "I eat it all the time." He looked rather like a cartoon: his hair was very curly and stood straight up on his head; he had an enormous thin nose and a pointed chin, and he was wearing long pointed shoes on his long skinny legs. He also had a lisp.

"Where were you Saturday?" Margaret asked me. Next to Albert she seemed surprisingly unexceptional: a large plump dark-haired woman in a black dress.

"My goodness, there was such a crush," I said girlishly. "No one could find anyone, could they?"

"We waited for you for forty minutes," Margaret remarked lugubriously.

"We couldn't even get into the lobby," I said.

"We waited in the lobby," Margaret replied.

"The reason I eat garlic," Albert explained, "is that it purifies the blood. It's very healthy. It counteracts the poisons."

He told us what poisons all the way to Bayswater where Maud Tweak lived. I was looking forward to seeing her apartment; somehow I had gotten the impression that it would exhibit sophisticated modern British decor. The minicab stopped in a rather crummy street outside a shop. "What's this?" I asked, confused.

"It's Maud's place," Margaret said.

"Oh, isn't she lucky to have it?" Albert cried.

"Oh, dreadfully lucky," Margaret remarked.

We went up to a little door next to the shop, and they rang the bell. It was a sort of antique shop, filled with queer odds and ends. Through the window I could see a school clock, a pine chest, and a very large doll with long yellow hair and staring china blue eyes, dressed in yellowed ruffles.

"This sort of thing is becoming all the rage in London now," Margaret said obscurely.

"We have this section called Old Town, in Chicago," I said.

The door opened suddenly. A small, very thin woman with sharp features stood before us. Her brown hair was bouffant, she was wearing silver slippers and a pretty blue dress with white dots. She radiated friendliness and warmth.

"Oh, my dear," she cried, seizing my hands, "I'm so happy to meet you. I'm Maud Tweak of course. Oh, do come in."

We climbed up four or five floors to a small attic apartment. From the hallway I could see the tiny sitting room: an interesting modern painting made a bright splash of color over the low fireplace next to built-in bookshelves and desk.

"Oh, it's charming!" I said. I had found the rather musty atmosphere of London so oppressive that the least touch of lightness and freshness sent me into an ecstasy. I understood too well Mark's fascination with the Playboy kitchen. The rest of the furniture was an old settee, painted white and furnished with cushions apparently made of cement, and two armless modern armchairs slipcovered in striped rayon.

We settled down and Maud poured wine for everyone. "I'm so delighted to meet you," she said to me. "How are the children?"

"Michael got his comeuppance the other day," Albert said happily.

"Oh, good," Maud replied. "What happened?"

"He was playing in the area and a man came by, the father of one of the children. Michael hit the boy, and the father spoke to him, and Michael called him a silly twit."

I was on top of this: Michael was Margaret's son, the same age as Eric.

"Called the *father?*" Maud said.

"Yes, and then Michael ran upstairs and the man followed him. He knocked on the door, and Michael hid. But I dragged him out, and the man gave him a tongue-lashing, and I put him to bed without supper."

Everyone laughed, except Jordan and me.

"Oh, marvelous," Maud said.

"Yes," Albert lisped. "I'm so pleased the man followed it through."

"I am too," Margaret said. "He could simply have let it go."

"Yes, he could," Maud remarked. "Awfully good job he didn't."

"Children should be struck regularly, like gongs," Albert said, and launched into a Swiftian discussion of child behavior. With his hooked nose, tall frizzy hair, long pointed shoes turned out on his thin ankles, to say nothing of his lisp and his habit of delivering pronouncements, he seemed to have stepped from the pages of the early Evelyn Waugh. I had been delighted with these creations during my long period of Anglophilia, now fast waning. I had never expected to *meet* one. I didn't know they were *real*.

"Michael's going to boarding school in the fall anyway," Margaret said.

"Oh, wonderful," Maud said enthusiastically. 'That'll straighten him out."

"Away from Mama," Albert said joyously, "it's sink or swim. No one to pat the head...."

From there they moved on to a discussion of a recent act of Margaret's which they considered monstrous: she had had an operation performed on someone named Tom, who turned out, to my relief, to have been her cat. Albert was exquisitely witty about it, Maud was gleeful, and Margaret castigated herself good-naturedly.

"But they spray the walls," I said, to help Margaret out. Nobody paid any attention to me except Jordan, who gave me a funny look. They talked about the cat for a while longer and then Maud went to a small table in the corner and began to serve dinner: egg salad, cold cuts and sliced tomatoes.

"Your vegetables here are delicious," I said sincerely. "I can't get enough tomatoes."

"How was Russia?" Albert said to Maud.

"Oh, thrilling," she replied. They began a swift geographical conversation, travelling rapidly from Russia to Scotland; they talked faster and faster, cutting each other off. I heard something about the Outer Hebrides.

"Wait a minute," I said. "Hold it. I'm lost. What are you talking about?"

Maud and Albert paused and looked at me.

"We're talking about the last war," Maud said. "I was stationed in Scotland, and I was ill there. The people were so kind, so thoughtful. That is the reason," she said, turning to Albert and sipping her wine, "that I shall *never* sneer at the people of the Outer Hebrides." She paused for an effect and went on. "I was in Dublin for my leaves. Of course there was one ball after another. I remember one evening I went to a ball at the German Embassy. I danced with the most *divine* young man. He said, 'What do you do?' and I said, 'Actually, darling, I'm in the British Army.'" She turned to me. "What do you think of your expatriates?" she asked abruptly.

I couldn't think of anyone except Henry James and T.S. Eliot.

"Your expatriates," she repeated. "What do you think of them? Bill, for instance. He's awfully funny, you know. I asked him how long he plans to live here and he said, 'For the rest of my life, I hope.'" She laughed.

"Yes, he likes it here," I said, smiling.

"I asked him what he liked so much," Maud said. "He said, 'Your parks. Your theater.'"

She and Margaret and Albert exploded into hearty laughter at this, and we smiled again, to be polite, although we didn't see anything funny about it. The London parks were beautiful, and there was a lot of good theater at good prices. When Jordan and I had been in London two years before, we had seen five plays in five days and enjoyed them all.

"I never go to the theater," Maud said. "No real Londoner does, you know."

"I don't think it's a very good season this year," I said, trying to be tactful.

Maud gave me a swift look. "Is it a good season in New York?" she asked sharply.

I really didn't know. "Those expatriates," Maud said to Albert. "You remember that dreadful cow that was here last month? Looked through my books and said some of them were on the Index. Dreadful cow." She looked at me. "She was travelling on an Irish passport. But she was one of your expatriates."

"Why was she on an Irish passport?"

"Oh, I suppose she hung round them and pestered them to death so they gave her one."

"But don't you have to be a citizen to get a passport?"

"Oh, they're not all that stuffy about it. She kept after them and they gave her an Irish passport to get rid of her. Stupid creature. And that friend of hers spilled wine all over the carpet."

"I don't have any desire to travel," Margaret said to me. "I've been to all the places worth seeing, and if anyone told me they'd give me a trip, I couldn't think of a place I wanted to see."

"Have you been to America?" I asked, stepping into it.

"No, I haven't," she said, smiling at me.

"We discovered a place to swim practically across the street from us," I said to Maud. "In the Serpentine."

"Pronounce it Serpentyne," she said.

"Serpentyne," I repeated. "We bought bathing suits at Woolworth's and it's been raining ever since."

"It's the rain that makes the flowers and vegetables so good," Jordan remarked.

"Oh, the raw materials are excellent," Albert said. "But what's done with them! Do you realize that I have had to give up eating canned peas because they're filled with green lead dye?"

"But they can't be," I said. "The government…"

"Ah, yes," Albert said. "Your government protects you with the Food and Drug laws. We don't have that kind of protection here. There are poisons, poisons, everywhere."

"Green lead dye," I said.

"Don't take any notice of him," Maud said kindly to me. "He's mad."

"As a good socialist," Albert said to Maud, "you ought to concern yourself with legislation against this sort of thing. I'm afraid to eat anything except garlic. It purifies the blood." He leaned back in his chair and looked at us, his great nose trembling with emotion.

"Of course change is coming," Maud remarked.

"Oh, change comes, everywhere," Albert said. "I mean actually the whole world is changing. For instance," he went on, "we've dropped all our nineteenth-century social snobberies in England since the war. And I suppose," he said graciously to us, "that in about two hundred years America will catch up to us, and drop *her* nineteenth-century class distinctions."

"We don't have nineteenth-century class distinctions in America," I said.

"No…" Maud poured wine into everybody's glass. "… you have distinctions based on money." She gave us a sympathetic smile. "It's awful," she said, wrinkling her nose at me.

"Yes," I said, "our distinctions are based on money, for the most part."

"I think rigid class distinctions are worse than money snobberies," Jordan observed.

Maud and Albert exchanged quick glances; Maud smiled.

"A lot of you Americans come over here," she said, "and run up bills at Fortnum's and Harrod's and all the big shops. Of course they don't have a bean. We just sit back and watch 'em till we're tired of them and then," she concluded with noticeable ferocity, "we dump 'em back!"

There was a really long pause after this remark.

"My goodness," I said, looking at my watch, "nearly eleven! We've really got to go."

We went into the bedroom to collect my coat.

"I just love your apartment," I said.

"And I did it all myself," Maud responded proudly.

"And it was so kind of you to have us."

"Well, it's meeting people, you know," she said.

22

Lunch

ON FRIDAY MORNING, Mrs. Grail arrived, brandishing an envelope. "Ah, the cheek," she cried, as soon as she got in the door. "The cheek of her! It came this morning. Burn it, my husband says, she's got no claim on you, she doesn't pay your wages."

"But what is it, Mrs. Grail?"

"Read it," she said, stuffing the envelope into my hand. "Ah, it's Them. The cheek of them, they'll do you every time."

The letter was from Mrs. Stackpole. It began with many expressions of hope for Mrs. Grail's health and well-being. Then:

> I do hope the Family are not proving too much for you. I hear they disagree a lot. I am so anxious to have you with me when I return, dear Mrs. Grail, I hope you will not hold me responsible for them. I shall be in London the last week in July. Please write and tell me whether I shall come to you, or when you can come to me. I am so anxious to talk with you.

"What does she mean, we disagree a lot?" I said indignantly. "Among ourselves or with other people?

"Ah, the wicked thing," Mrs. Grail said. "I'll never see her, I'll never write to her."

"I suppose Miss Pip said something," I said. "I suppose she said we're disagreeable people."

"Ah, you're not. I'll do for you until you leave, until September fourth. But I'll never work for her, never."

"My husband has to stay until September because of his business," I said, looking through the window at the gray street. "I mean actually the children and I don't have to stay that long really."

"Well, I'll do for him then, the dear man," Mrs. Grail said. She seized the letter which I had vaguely thought of preserving for a lawsuit involving invasion of privacy and libel or something, and tore it to fragments. "That's for her," she said, "the horrid, horrid thing!"

I went upstairs and reported Mrs. Stackpole's latest perfidy to Jordan, who was dressing to go to the office.

"She's kind of awful," he said weakly.

"*Kind* of awful!" I cried. "She's a big fink. Spying on us. Isn't there a law against that?"

"Don't know," he said.

"Can't you ask your lawyer?"

He gave me a hopeless glance.

"Well, can't you?"

"It wouldn't do any good to ask him."

"What do you mean?"

"Those people in Birmingham are supposed to call this week," he said, changing the subject. "Maybe they'll buy into the business."

"And if they don't?"

"Oh, I guess they will. But if they don't, Basil said he would do something."

"What can Basil do?"

"I don't know. *Something,*"he said, with a note of hysteria in his voice. He made an effort to calm himself, and asked, "What are you going to do today?"

"Well, we went to the Comedy Theatre the other day—Eric calls it the Comedy Feeler, isn't that funny?—but the show only lasts an hour, it's hardly worth the trip. Except the trip takes up time too, which is good. But it's right near Madame Tussaud's, and it makes Eric nervous to be so near Madame Tussaud's, so I'm not sure we ought to go to the Comedy Theatre again."

"Well, don't then."

"Mark said he would like to go to Madame Tussaud's, but I don't see how I can take him there with Eric feeling like this."

"I'm sure you can work it out," Jordan said

"I don't think I can work things out much longer," I said. "I'm going crazy."

"Maybe we can go to the country again," Jordan said. "It's bound to be better next time."

"At least I'm glad Mark is going to spend the day with us today. He's practically an adult; he can share things, you know."

"I wish he'd be a little more adult around the office," Jordan said gloomily. "He keeps making copies of Beatle pictures on the copy machine."

Mark and Bruce were insistent upon going to Madame Tussaud's; Mark had not yet been there. So we went to Baker Street on the bus. They went to Madame Tussaud's and Eric and I went to the Comedy Feeler where they were showing a Laurel and Hardy movie which did not amuse him or anyone else in the audience, for that matter. Eric squirmed in his seat; he kept glancing at the entrance.

"Let's go," he said after ten minutes.

"We have to stay here until it's over," I said. "We're giving Mark and Bruce an hour at… at… the place where they are, and this movie runs for an hour."

"Where are they?" Eric asked in a throaty whisper.

"You know where they are," I said testily. "They're at Madame Tussaud's. Watch the movie."

"Madame Tussaud's is right down the street," Eric said.

"I know it."

"Let's get out of here."

"They're made of wax," I said, for the fifteenth time. "They're not real. They can't leave the building. Watch the movie."

"I want to go."

"We have to wait."

"Why?" I threw in the towel and we left and stood outside Madame Tussaud's, a location that Eric for some reason found preferable to the Feeler, for fifteen or twenty minutes, until Mark and Bruce emerged, full of praise for the slot machines.

"Gosh, is that cool," Mark said. "There's nothing like that in Chicago."

"No," I said loudly, for Eric's benefit, "there is no Wax Museum in Chicago."

"I mean those slot machines," Mark said. "Boy, are those cool."

"Did you see Hamlet's uncle?" Eric asked.

"I love slot machines," Bruce said. "I love them more than anything in the world. I just lost sixpence. Wow," he added, reaching for one, "look at the Beatle magazines."

"'ere," growled a Cockney voice, "get your filthy 'ands off them books."

"Did you hear what he said to me?" Bruce said.

"Did you see Hamlet's uncle?"

"I'm starving," Mark said, "let's get lunch."

"Lots of luck," I said crossly.

"Why are you so contrary?" Mark said to me. "You always expect the worst. Look at this, let's go in here, this chicken place."

"It looks good," Bruce said. "Did you hear what that man said to me?"

We went into the chicken restaurant, which was crowded because it was lunchtime, and sat at a large table. There were all sorts of relatively fresh stains on the tablecloth.

"Could we have a clean tablecloth, please?" I said to the waiter.

"What do you want to eat?" he countered.

"I want a clean tablecloth," I said loudly.

He glared at me for a minute and then two sub-waiters came up with two halves of a clean tablecloth and put them together on the table.

"What do you want?" the waiter said.

"Well, I'll have the fried fish, and Mark, do you want the fried fish too? Yes, we'll both have fried fish with fried potatoes."

Bruce said he wasn't hungry; all he wanted was some ice cream.

At this point the waiter went away to take someone else's order.

"What a rude waiter," I said. After five or ten minutes, the waiter came back. "That will be two fried fish," I said. "And a fried chicken dinner for the little boy, with mashed potatoes if you have them."

The waiter went off to seat somebody.

"He's getting impossible," I said.

"You shouldn't have asked for the clean tablecloth," Mark told me.

"Why not?" I asked. "They wouldn't want to serve on a dirty tablecloth, would they?"

We both knew they would, so Mark didn't answer. The waiter returned, looking very hostile.

"We'll have two fried fish dinners," I said, "and one fried chicken dinner for the little boy, and cokes all around, and this little boy will just have ice cream, he doesn't want a dinner."

The waiter became very agitated and put his pad away.

"You'll have to leave," he said. "We're too busy here to bother with people who want ice cream. All of you will have to have a dinner or else you'll all have to leave."

"I'm not very hungry," Bruce said apologetically.

"Well!" I said to Mark, who was staring at me. "There you go. We'll leave."

Mark continued to stare at me. "Things like that never happen to me when I'm by myself," he said. "It must be your fault. It must have something to do with all of you."

"But what did we do?" I asked, getting up. "We didn't do anything."

"I know you didn't seem to do anything," Mark said, as we walked out. "But I go around everywhere all day for Dad, and things like that never happen to me, so you must be doing something."

"But *what* are we doing that's wrong?"

"Besides," he added logically, "that waiter wasn't even English. He was some kind of Yugoslav or something."

We went to a hamburger restaurant and ate the gray meat with muddy gravy out of square metal dishes.

23

The Wallace Collection

AFTER WE FINISHED LUNCH, I suggested we walk down to the Wallace Collection.

"I don't think it's very far from here. Your father and I loved it when we were here the first time. Our hotel was right around the comer from the Wallace Collection; I can show it to you afterward."

"Let's take a cab," Mark said.

"I think we should walk. It's not raining for a change. Let's stroll down."

We asked the waiter in the hamburger place how far it was to Manchester Square. He said it was a ten-minute walk. I explained to the children that English people reckoned distances in terms of time because they didn't have our geometrical block system.

"Also they don't have our attitude toward walking," Mark said. "Ten minutes means half an hour."

We strolled off and just as we began to fail physically, we came upon Manchester Square.

"There it is," I cried triumphantly. "That wasn't so bad, was it?"

"I have a stomachache," Bruce said.

"My feet hurt," Mark said.

"I feel good, I want to see the Museum," Eric said. "Are there any wax figures there?"

"No, of course not," I replied irritably. "Do you think I'd ever take you to see wax figures again? There's some really lovely armor and some beautiful pictures... and the building itself...."

"Oh, goody, armor," Eric said. "I love armor."

We went inside.

"I feel sick," Bruce said. "My stomach hurts. I want to go home."

"We've come this far," I said. "Why not look at it? You'll love it."

"Just a lot of pictures and some armor?" Mark asked.

"And the building itself," I said. "Look around. And some French furniture, of course."

"Oh, furniture, furniture," Bruce said. "That's all you care about, furniture."

"Why don't you smack him one?" Mark asked.

"My feet hurt, my stomach hurts, and all you care about is furniture," Bruce said.

"Let's try to be quiet," I said. "Everyone is looking at us. Oh, my, look at this beautiful painting. And what do you think of this clock?"

"If I ever talked to you that way, you'd smack me," Mark said.

"I have to go to the bathroom," Bruce said.

"Ask the man," I said.

"I want to see the armor," Eric said sweetly. "Oh, what a lovely place."

"Eric likes this place," I said, eyeing him suspiciously.

"If I don't sit down, I'm going to faint," Mark said.

"I don't think you should sit there," I said.

"Why not? There's no cord over it or anything. It's a chair, isn't it?"

"Here, you can't sit there," a guard cried, darting forward. "You can't sit on that chair."

"I told you," I said.

"I'm going to faint," Mark said.

"Shall we go upstairs? They've got Gainsboroughs...."

"How can I look at paintings when I'm going to faint?"

"Oh, here's Bruce," I said cheerfully. "Feeling better?"

"No, I'm not," Bruce said, scowling. "I feel worse. My stomach hurts and I want to sit down."

"Why don't you both go out in the courtyard and sit on a bench?" I suggested. "I'll show Eric the armor."

I showed Eric the armor for quite a while. He seemed to admire it.

"Oh, look at the big horse," he said. "Look at the armor on the big horse. Look at the big curved sword. Did they cut off people's heads with it?"

"That must have been the intention," I replied. "See how beautifully it's carved?"

"I have to go to the bathroom," Eric said suddenly.

"Oh, dear. It's right down that way, I think."

"I can't go by myself. I'm afraid of Hamlet's uncle."

"Hamlet's uncle isn't in the bathroom. I mean the lavatory. He isn't anywhere. I mean he's in Madame Tussaud's.... No, he isn't, I didn't mean that—"

"I want Mark to go with me," Eric said loudly.

"Shhh," I said.

We sought Mark out where he sat in the courtyard with Bruce on an institutional-looking oak bench. It was drizzling.

"I want to go home," Bruce said.

"Shhh," I said. "Eric has to go to the bathroom."

"So what?" Mark said.

"Shhh. He wants you to go with him, Mark. He's afraid."

"He's afraid? In broad daylight? In a museum?"

"I'm afraid of Hamlet's uncle," Eric said.

"You are *not*," Mark said.

"He is too," I said.

"He's crazy," Mark said.

"That's beside the point," I replied. "The point is, the child is frightened and you're old enough to understand, you're sixteen years old...."

"Hurry *up*," Eric said.

"Why am I only fifteen if I want to do something interesting and sixteen if you want me to do something?"

"You're all crazy," Bruce said. "Look at that man staring at us."

"Mark!" I said.

"Oh, all right. Come on, you miserable hateful little brat."

"Mommy!" Eric called back loudly. "He's pulling me!"

"Shhh. Stop pulling him."

Bruce and I were left alone in the drizzle.

"You see this interesting courtyard," I said. "This used to be somebody's house, imagine that, and the lady left it as a museum to the public. These horrible benches were not here when the lady lived here, of course. It must have been beautiful then."

"I'm getting all wet," Bruce said.

"I can't help it," I responded testily.

"Yes, you could too help it," Bruce said. "We didn't have to come to this awful place."

"What awful place? England?"

"No, not England. I love England. You hate it, but I love it. I mean *this* awful place."

"I thought you would like it," I said sadly.

"Well, I don't," Bruce said. He got up and went back to the lavatory. I sat on the bench in the rain and read one of Mark's rock and roll magazines until they all came back.

"Do you want to go upstairs?" I asked.

Eric said he did. Suddenly I felt rather tired.

"We'll do it next time," I said. "Let's go."

We walked around the corner and passed the hotel where Jordan and I had stayed on our first visit to London. I pointed it out to the children; it looked much better to me than it had the first time.

"Oh, it's lovely, Mommy," Eric said. "Can we stay there now?"

"Hey, it's cool," Mark said.

"You stayed in this awful dump?" Bruce asked. "What for?"

24

Plumbing

SEVERAL DAYS HAD ELAPSED, and the water was still streaming down the lavatory wall. Mrs. Grail alternated between telling me to leave it for Mrs. Stackpole, whom she kept seeing slinking around Knightsbridge, and urging me to do something so that Mrs. Stackpole would not fly into a vindictive rage and do something terrible to us. I had heard neither from the plumber nor from Mr. MacAllister. I decided to try the plumber again.

"He's away on holiday," the woman said.

"But this is an emergency. Isn't there someone else I could call?"

"When he returns, I'll send him round."

"But water has been coming down the wall for *days!* Can't you give me another name to call? Isn't there anyone else there?"

"I've already told you, Madam. When... he... returns...."

I hung up and told Mrs. Grail about it.

"At home," I said, close to tears, "at home plumbers are listed in the phone book. They have emergency numbers. Here, they're all on vacation at the same time...."

"Ah, the cheeky things," Mrs. Grail said.

I tried to call Mr. MacAllister.

"He's away on holiday," the girl said.

The doorbell rang. It was the laundry man.

"Oh," I said. "It's two o'clock and the last time Mrs. Grail said you came after two. You see, she leaves at two, and the girl in the office said you would be here *before* two."

"They don't know nuffink in the office," he said, growling.

"Well. Still. If you could manage to be here before two…"

"I can't know what time I can be here." He was becoming upset. "'Be here then, be here now.' It's all I can do to get all them calls. What do you think I am? I can't make promises, I can't say this or that. I'm not going to be picked at, they don't know nuffink in the office."

"Oh, forget it," I said. "Calm down."

"'Be here now, then go there.'" He thrust a pamphlet into my hand. "I already said I didn't know what time. I can't kill myself, I won't."

"I said forget it," I said, looking at the pamphlet. "What's this?"

"That's your *book,*" he said, scowling horribly. "Don't lose it."

"But what is it?"

"It's your *book.*" He went out, slamming the door hard behind him.

"What a rude man," I said to Mrs. Grail, who was in the basement putting her coat on.

"Ah, it's the English. They're all like that."

"What is this thing he gave me?"

Mrs. Grail looked at it. "Ah, that's your book, dear. Don't lose it."

"But what is it?"

"It's your book," Mrs. Grail said.

I went upstairs and phoned Jordan. "And Mr. MacAllister is out," I said. "Everyone is away on holiday. What on earth are we going to do about the water? Call the fire department?"

"Maybe I should look up a plumber in the directory," he said.

"You mean you *have* one?"

"They're given to businesses."

"Why on earth didn't you tell me this before? The carpet is soaked, the paint is blistered…."

"Please," he said, "don't bug me. I'm going crazy. If Basil Goldbrick doesn't buy into this goddamn thing, we'll sneak out of the country under cover of darkness."

"Well, if we have to leave, we have to leave." I thought of what it would be like to be at home: the sun would be shining brightly, I could wear a cotton dress and no coat, the children could play outside. I could buy real meat and cook it on a real stove. "We'll just have to make the best of it," I said gamely.

While I was putting the book in a safe place, Jordan phoned to say a plumber was coming the next day. "I called a place in Chelsea. It says Plumbers and Decorators. I guess it's all right."

"Thank God," I said. There was moss growing on the downstairs bathroom floor.

"I don't know what's wrong with these people here," Jordan said, referring to the office. "One of the ladies has an upper-class accent and she keeps ordering the others around. She sits and tells them to get things for her."

"I suppose they do it."

"Yes, how do you know that?"

"Oh, I just sort of know." A month in the British Isles was giving me all sorts of knowledge. I kept thinking about all those English novels I had read, and all the English movies

I had seen. I remembered how we had thought that opening a business in England was a splendid idea; we might want to move there someday....

* * *

The next day was the last day of camp. I went with the boys to West Ruyslip on the underground. That took an hour. I left them there and set off for North Lambeth to retrieve Eric's sweater and raincoat. This trip took more than an hour. I sat next to a young man in sneakers. He had a large duffel bag with him, with a Canadian flag on it.

"I'm just going back," he said, sniffling. "I was on my way to France and I forgot my passport. Now I have to go all the way back and get it. I'm a Canadian," he said unnecessarily. "I live in Montreal. I'm going to spend the summer in Europe. What do you think of London?"

"Well..."

"They don't like you because you're an American. Americans are hated everywhere. That's why I have that flag on my bag. I don't want to be mistaken for an American. It's so damp here," he said, sneezing. "I caught a cold. I've been here a week and I caught a cold, and now I have to go to France. After that I'm going to Germany and Austria, and then I'm going to Italy, to Rome. I have an audience with the Pope." He sneezed again.

"It sounds interesting," I said. "You're lucky."

He nodded without enthusiasm. "I wish it was over," he said.

He leaped up, seized his bag, waved at me and charged out. I travelled the rest of the way to North Lambeth in silence. When I finally got there, I found the police station after several errors and climbed the stairs to confront a man in a glass cage, like a movie theater cashier. Since I knew the day and even the hour of the loss, the man went straight to a cubby hole and redeemed the items, wrapped in brown paper and tied with heavy string.

"Oh, good," I said, reaching for the parcel.

The policeman held onto it. "We charge two shillings a pound of the worth of the item," he said. "It's a reward to the driver for turning it in."

It became clear to me why the driver had not stopped when Bruce called to him, and why he had not checked the seat after his juvenile passengers.

"Would you say the items are worth ten pounds?" the man asked.

"No," I said churlishly. "I got them at Marks and Spencer."

"All right, five pounds?"

They weren't worth five pounds, or roughly twelve dollars, but I couldn't remember what I had paid for them. I ended up paying nine shillings in a state of total confusion and feeling like a liar.

"It's to reward the driver," the policeman called after me, "for his honesty."

I walked back about five blocks to the underground and travelled hastily to Baldridge Place to see what the plumbers were doing. They said that the trouble stemmed from the Children's Bathroom, unheated, but with darling decals of Little Bo-Peep and Little Mary Quite Contrary all over the wall, which was peeling. The tub had a telephone shower, an awkward contrivance that you hold in your hand. Since it was the only shower in the house, Mark and I had used it to wash our hair.

The plumber said that the bathtub drain was defective and the tub was not properly caulked. We had never filled the tub, but of course the telephone shower emptied into the drain, so we decided that that was what was causing the leak. We were rather suspicious of the toilet, too, so we called the entire Children's Bathroom out of bounds. It did have an airing cupboard ("There's your airing cupboard," Mrs. Stackpole had said proudly), an entity I remembered from my days of reading Elizabeth Bowen and Rosamond Lehmann. Apparently some hot water pipes travelled through it, and you were supposed to put things in there to dry them out. It was fully as damp as the rest of the house; maybe a little damper.

We were now reduced to one bathroom: ours. Since it was on the second floor or two flights up from the basement kitchen by American count, we were all rather put out, especially since Eric always had to go to the bathroom during meals and television programs and he refused to go up alone because of Hamlet's father, and also because of the wax Queen Mother, whose beady little eyes seemed to follow him still.

25

Roof Garden and Knees

THE SATURDAY MORNING rolled around when we had arranged to meet Althea on the roof of Derry & Tom's department store. When I arrived with the children at the appointed time of eleven o'clock, Althea was there with her sister, a plain, pleasant person in a dark raincoat. Althea apologized for asking us to meet so early; the roof closed at one o'clock on Saturday.

We bought tickets from a woman ticket taker stationed at a table near the elevator, or lift, and walked quickly through the garden to the restaurant. There were bushes, flowers and trees growing amid fountains, stone benches and Tudor archways, high above the city.

"You haven't seen anything like this before, have you?" Althea asked.

"No, I haven't."

She smiled. "I daresay it's the only one of its kind in the world," she said.

The restaurant was light, airy and very clean. We adults ordered croissants and coffee, which was very good; Bruce and Eric had milk with their croissants, and Mark had a chocolate sundae, produced to his satisfaction without any problem. This time, I thought gratefully, we were in luck. It really was a charming restaurant. Althea said that during the week, salads were served there for lunch. She said this was an American innovation that was beginning to catch on.

"How have you been getting on?" Althea asked me.

"Well," I said, "there isn't very much to do, and the weather's been awful. We've had some trouble with the landlady. Actually," I said, surprising myself, "I wish we could get away for a while. I'd like to go somewhere. I'd like to go to Paris," I said, dreamily. "I was there once for five days; it was so beautiful. And the food... but of course you've been there. I mean you're so near to France."

"Oh, dear no," Althea said. "I've never been there. I've never been out of England. I wouldn't go there, I wouldn't dream of it. All those foreigners, all those strange customs."

I looked at her. "It's a very common English attitude," her sister said, smiling. "You'll find it's not at all unusual."

"I should like to go to America," Althea said. "I'd enjoy that. But those foreigners. Oh, dear, no, I couldn't stand it."

"Well," I said, "anyway, I'd like to go somewhere. But travelling is so expensive."

"Why don't you go to Devon and Cornwall?" Althea suggested. "It's beautiful."

"Oh yes," her sister said. "Devon. It's lovely there. Motor down, and travel through."

"You'd love it," Althea said. "You really should see the English countryside."

After we finished lunch, it was twelve-thirty.

"We'd better hurry," Althea said. "The roof closes at one."

We all went out into the gardens and Althea began to point out flowers and little pools with fishes in them. We followed her. Suddenly a Boy came up, with a snub nose and a funny accent, like a Boy in Dickens.

"Excuse me, Madam," he said to Althea. "But the roof is closed now."

"No, it isn't," Althea said. "It closes at one, and it's only twenty-five to."

"Well, excuse me, Madam," the Boy said, "but you have to go down now."

"Look at this precious statue," Althea said. "It's a copy of one in Florence."

She began to walk about in a carefree sort of way, and we followed her nervously, with the Boy beside us. Her sister hung back near the elevator. Or lift.

"Here, Madam," the Boy said. "Come on then."

"Don't take any notice of him," Althea said to me. "It's like this *every* week." She stopped to admire a stone arch with a sort of face carved into it.

"It's all authentic, you know," she said to Mark. "It's all copied from authentic things in old gardens."

"Madam," the Boy said.

"Isn't it lovely?" Althea asked. She turned to the Boy. "It's no good following us about," she said. "We're going to stay. Look at those people, they're still eating. How can the gardens close?" She gestured toward the restaurant, where we could see people sitting at umbrella tables on the wide veranda. I couldn't help thinking she had a good point there.

"You've got to go down now," the Boy said stubbornly. "Silly old clot," he murmured.

"What's wrong with them?" the ticket taker said shrilly, gathering up her belongings. "Inconsiderate, I call it."

"Well, they won't come," the Boy said. The elevator door was open; the elderly male operator stood at the ready, looking irritated.

"It's no good waiting," Althea said. "We're not going yet. It's not even ten of."

"Listen, Madam," the Boy said, "I'm going to call the guards. How would you like that?"

"Oh, go away," Althea said. "My friends from America want to see the gardens." The children and I were miserably pacing behind her, casting longing looks at the elevator, or lift. The sun shone brightly down on us; palm trees waved in the breeze.

"What do you think of these palm trees?" Althea asked.

"Now get out of this," the Boy said angrily. "I've 'ad enough. Come on, get out of it."

"Althea," I said.

"Well," Althea said. She stopped and looked around. "We've seen enough." She turned to the Boy. "We're going because *we're* ready," she said with dignity. "We've seen enough. But it's not one o'clock yet. I know the roof closes at one."

"Oh, get out," the Boy said.

We got into the elevator with the silent operator, and were taken down. The Boy came with us.

"Now leave the store," he said, when we got out.

"Oh, shut up," Althea said.

We walked through parts of Kensington with Althea, seeing Holland Park and lovely little alleys with shops in them.

"There's the Commonwealth Institute," Althea said, pointing to a really beautiful modern building. "You must take the children there, they have movies."

Eric bought a carton of milk at a milk machine and we parted from Althea and her sister.

When I got home, I phoned Jordan, who was at the office, still struggling with Pressclips U.K. "Basil Goldbrick is definitely in, I think," he asserted, without much conviction.

"Well, thank God for that," I replied fervently, thinking that we might then be able to leave town for anywhere.

"Listen," he said tensely, "I think we should give a party."

"Urk," I said. He had mentioned this before.

"I know. But after all, Basil and Daisy have taken me out for dinner several times and we do have the house and I think we should use it. Besides, Walter and Nini will be here." That was true: Walter and Nini were friends from Chicago, who were going to spend a few days in London before pushing off for Holland, Nini's native land.

"All right," I said.

Jordan invited Basil and Daisy and Maud Tweak and Margaret. He also invited Albert, who couldn't come, and a couple of public relations people, who could. This was Saturday and the party was set for the following Friday evening. Walter and Nini arrived on Monday, and we went to dinner with them. They appeared in our musty entrance hall, relics of Chicago. I felt as though I were seeing them under water.

Life in general had taken on a strange dream-like quality. Every day we rose, washed and ate, and then the boys and I went out and wandered around: we went to Harrods or we went to Selfridge's on some trumped-up errand like buying a school satchel; if the sun was shining we went to Regent's Park and the children travelled around and around the pond in a motor boat. Sometimes we went to Hyde Park so that they could play ball or dabble their feet in the Serpentine, a remarkably filthy stream. In the evening I would take home a little roast or some terrible steak or fatty hamburger or excellent fish and cook it on the New World while soot dropped from the old chimney. I would wash the dishes watching people's legs go by the kitchen window; the glasses were always streaky and faintly coated with grease. I tore my stockings on the orange crate benches Mrs. Stackpole had provided for kitchen dining, and every Thursday we remembered to wind the boiler so it would not blow up.

We wandered the city, on foot, on buses, on the underground, or Tube, and in taxicabs. Twice I saw people reading books: a man walked down the street reading a Mickey Spillane, another man in the cab of a truck was reading Earl Stanley Gardiner. A thin woman on a bus called the children "brats" and got off in an incomprehensible fury; another woman shouted at a grocer for thrusting her package at her in an insolent manner, and the grocer shouted back, and in the supermarket in Knightsbridge which I frequented, a dowager lost her temper with the cashier for taking the money of the next person in line before the dowager had finished bagging her own purchases. I had great difficulty adjusting to this system myself: you frantically stuffed your groceries into your sack while customers behind you stepped on your heels and glared at you because they needed space to stuff *their* groceries into *their* sacks.

The buses were of course packed in the rush hour, but there was a rule that no one was allowed to stand in the aisles upstairs, and only a designated number were allowed to stand downstairs. The aged or infirm were not permitted to climb the stairs. Once we saw a very old, crippled man get on a bus with a young woman. The conductor said, "Five seats upstairs. No one can stand down here." The young woman steered her aged companion toward the stairs. The conductor blocked his way. "You can't go upstairs," he said. Several women, including me, offered their seats to the old gentleman in an agitated flurry.

Tempers were short in the city despite the cool weather, but perhaps because of the incessant rain; I heard that this was the rainiest summer in forty-five years. Prices were very high indeed, things cost as much as they did in America, but wages were low by American standards. Living conditions were by and large uncomfortable. An aura of antiquity hung over London; I found it oppressive. I had always had a romantic predilection for the past; now I felt as though I were in a city where time was trapped anywhere between 1900 and 1937. And this despite the Mod influence, which seemed to exist only for the young.

I went happily into a Mary Quant shop in Knightsbridge, where I was surrounded by willowy young things with projecting hipbones and giraffe-like necks. "Am I the only one in here over twenty?" I said nervously to the salesgirl, or shop assistant.

"Actually, I'm twenty-three," she said evasively.

"But I mean, does anyone over twenty-five ever come in here?"

"Actually," she said, "no."

I went ahead anyway, and bought two dresses.

"At home, you know," I babbled, "at home, I mean in the United States, women wear anything they want to, at any age." I was trying desperately to convince her. "I daresay English women are more conservative," she said. "I suppose it's different in the States." The seamstress looked up at me disapprovingly. "How short do you want it, Madam? You don't want it too short, do you?"

"They seem to be wearing them quite short," I said.

"You don't want to show your knees, do you?" she asked.

"Everybody else is," I said defensively.

She didn't reply to that. "About like this, I think," she said, holding the hem carefully over my knee.

I gave it a stylish elevation. "How about like this?" I said.

Her lips compressed, she pulled it down again. "You don't want to show your knees," she said firmly. I had the feeling that if I protested, I would be shown out of the shop; I already felt that a woman of my advanced age (39) was there only on sufferance to begin with.

26

Evening Out

ON THURSDAY, we arranged to meet Walter and Nini at
the theater. I had not yet been to the theater because Jordan
had seen, walked out of, or fallen asleep during almost all the
London productions when he had been alone in the city all
winter. But we were going to see *The Killing of Sister George,* a
relatively new play that had gotten excellent reviews. As I was
getting ready to go, the phone rang.

"Mrs. Jordan Millah?" a rather bubbly voice screamed; it
could only be Mr. MacAllister.

"How are you, Mrs. Jordan Millah?" I think he thought
"Mrs. Jordan" was a title, like "the Right Honorable."

"I had a call here from your husband about the pipe," he
said. "I thought all that had been taken care of long ago."

"Well, no. We couldn't get a plumber, you see. We tried and
tried, and the water kept coming down."

Mr. MacAllister gave a sudden shriek of laughter.

"How awful for you," he said.

"Well, yes. We didn't know what to do. I called you and
I called the plumber and no one was there. Finally my husband looked it up in the directory. *He* has a directory, you see,
because he's in business."

"Oh, dear me," Mr. MacAllister said.

"Yes. So finally we got a plumber, but of course by that time the water had been coming down for quite a while, so I'm afraid the wall has to be repainted and the plumber had to chop a hole in the powder room ceiling to let the water out.. .."

"A hole," Mr. MacAllister said.

"Yes," I went on, unable to resist a rapt audience. "And of course the carpet was soaked, and he had to cut a hole because the ceiling was sagging, and he left a bucket—"

"Sagging," Mr. MacAllister said.

"—and he left a bucket on the toilet seat but no water is falling in, so I assume it's all right. We just can't use the Children's Bathroom because the tub has a defective drain."

"I think I'll just come round and see, shall I?"

"When?"

"Yes, I think I'll just pop round now."

"Well, I'm going out," I said. "To the theater, and I was just leaving."

"I'll just pop round," Mr. MacAllister said, with his ethnic persistence. "See you in five minutes."

I made a feeble attempt to get Mark to handle Mr. MacAllister so I could leave, but he kept insisting he wouldn't know what to say to him. Finally, after I spent fifteen minutes fretting on the front stoop in my dangling earrings and silk coat, a small sports car drove up and Mr. MacAllister emerged. He had popping pale blue eyes, colorless thinning hair combed straight back, two chins and a protruding stomach.

"Mrs. Jordan Millah?" he asked, as I stood on the stoop.

I took him down the hall to the powder room; he nearly dislocated his neck trying to peer inside the sitting room where the children were watching TV, such as it was, but I had closed the door nearly all the way. He looked at the blistered paint, the soaked carpet, the bulging ceiling with the hole in it. "Several hundred pounds worth of damage here, I should imagine," he said.

"Yes, it's too bad," I said.

He gave a sudden screech of laughter. I decided that this must be a nervous habit.

We went upstairs and he looked carefully around the Children's Bathroom. "It seems in order here," he said.

"Yes, but this is where the water came from. They pried up the floor boards and that's all dry; you see, we didn't use this bathroom. The water came from the defective drain. All we did was wash our hair with the telephone shower."

"But what did the plumber do?" Mr. MacAllister asked.

"He said not to use the tub."

He gave one of his screams. "How extr'ordin'ry," he said. "Didn't he *mend* it?"

"No, he didn't."

"But how *extr'ordin'ry!*" Another scream, ending in a hiccup.

"Well," I said tactfully."I'm late."

"D'you want a lift?"

"Oh, thanks," I said feeling that my lateness was his fault anyway. "I'm going to meet my husband at the St. George Theater. Do you know where that is?"

"No, actually I don't, but I'll find it." I climbed into Mr. MacAllister's little blue car, and we took off, almost literally.

"I can't understand it," he said. "Mrs. Stackpole's children were bathed regularly in that tub for months. By their Nanny," he added. "And nothing happened."

"Yes, well," I said. "Our children didn't use it."

I began to detect a note of recrimination; my hackles rose.

"But how did they *bathe?*" he asked. His tone implied doubt that they did.

"In our bathroom," I said, adding spitefully, "The Children's Bathroom is too cold."

This remark evoked another screech of laughter; we darted into traffic and cut off a large truck. The truck driver turned very red in the face and, leaning out of his window, he shouted something very nasty at Mr. MacAllister, who stared thoughtfully at the truck driver for a moment, and then rolled down his window and poked his own head out.

"What?" he called to the truck driver.

The truck driver turned even redder and repeated his insult with embellishments.

Mr. MacAllister laughed shortly. "Ha," he said to me. "That fellow. How extr'ordin'ry." Several horns were honking. We shoved off again, narrowly missing more cars, and weaving wildly about.

"I imagine," Mr. MacAllister said thoughtfully, "that that tub was filled to overflowing and allowed to remain that way for hours. I imagine that the water was left running for hours."

I had taken a very strong dislike to Mr. MacAllister and I was sitting with him in a little blue car that he obviously did not know how to drive; our knees were virtually touching.

"By whom?" I asked, grammatical to the end.

"By you," Mr. MacAllister said. "Or by your children."

"I have already told you," I said in a low voice with some controlled rage in it, "that we did not use that tub. Are you calling me a liar?"

Mr. MacAllister shrieked with laughter.

"Did you?" he said in a surprised voice. "Really?"

"Yes, I did," I said. "The tub had not been used; the plumber said the floor boards were dry; it never overflowed. Why don't you talk to the plumber?"

"I think I'll do that," Mr. MacAllister said.

He laughed again, very loudly. "I don't know what kind of plumber your husband called," he said. "The man is listed as a decorator."

"He was all we could find. We were sort of desperate."

I could have added a few choice words here, like I called you and you didn't help, but I didn't want to go into it.

"Here we are in Trafalgar Square," Mr. MacAllister said. "You say the theater is near here?"

"Somewhere," I said, spotting two policemen on the comer. "Perhaps we could ask."

"Do *you* mind asking?" Mr. MacAllister said. He stopped the car and after a moment I realized that he wanted me to get out. He sat behind the wheel while I crawled out and slammed the door. Then he whizzed off and left me near the curb, or kerb. The policemen, who looked to be about fourteen years old, looked up the theater in a book and after some difficulty directed me to it

I hobbled three blocks, or a six minute walk, in my elegant shoes. My face felt as though it were set in concrete, my earrings dangled with rage. "What's wrong?" Jordan said. "Why are you late? Why is your face so white? What happened?" I told him briefly, through stiff lips, that Mr. MacAllister had accused me of allowing the tub to overflow and then had dumped me out of his car in Trafalgar Square. "I'll call my lawyer," Jordan said. "Maybe we can break the lease. This is ridiculous."

Nini and Walter appeared. I told them about Mr. MacAllister.

"The English," Nini said "A few minutes ago here comes a boy and steps on my foot. He didn't even say he was sorry." She had always been an Anglophobe, and particularly disliked the Queen, for no discernible reason except a competitive preference for the Dutch royal family.

"How rude," I said.

We went into the theater and I watched the first act of the mediocre play; I think it was mediocre, I was mostly thinking about Mr. MacAllister. In the intermission, or interval, we went out into a very crowded bar. Two men and a woman were standing behind us; one of the men had long bushy sideburns, a sort of Oscar Wilde costume, and an expression of extreme arrogance. We chatted desultorily with Nini and Walter, sipping our drinks, until Oscar's companion, leaving the bar, apparently decided that Jordan was blocking his way. He unleashed an interestingly long arm and gave Jordan a tremendous shove; Walter, who was nearly seven feet tall, caught him before his nose hit the wall. Oscar Wilde and his two friends stared at us with lifted eyebrows. I felt like an eighteenth century peasant whose two-year-old had just been run over by the Squire's coach. We walked stiffly back to our seats, Oscar's drawl ringing in our ears. I heard the woman say loudly, "They must be Americans or something."

27

The Party

THE NEXT DAY I called Percy Snell, Jordan's lawyer, to tell
him that Mr. MacAllister had made sinister and insulting alle-
gations and I wanted to be protected from them. Percy Snell
laughed a good deal; he sounded exactly like Mr. MacAllister.
I began to wonder whether I could be losing my mind.

"I shouldn't worry about anything," Percy Snell said.

"Listen," I said slowly. "Can't we move out? I mean there
was a dining room table here when Jordan saw it first, and it
isn't here now. Can't we break the lease and move *out?*"

This sent Percy Snell into stitches. "Oh, you can't do that,"
he said. "I shouldn't think you could do that."

"But what about *harassment?*"

"I should think he just got nervous and lost his temper,"
Percy Snell said.

"But he *said* I spilled water all over the place and I *didn't.*"

"I expect he was upset."

I discussed this at some length with Jordan.

"First of all," he said, "I think we should go somewhere for
a vacation. I'd like," he said, in a dreamy voice, "I'd like some-
place warm. With a beach, a sandy beach. And the sun, the sun
shining all day long. On the hot sand."

"How about Glencoe, Illinois?" I asked, bitterly.

"And a hotel," he went on. "A beautiful hotel, very modern. Very, *very* modern. With balconies. With lots of glass. With carpets." There was a pause. We both remembered how we had whiled away many an American evening laughing our heads off at wall-to-wall carpeting and teak furniture.

"Oh, boy," I said faintly.

"We'll go down to American Express," Jordan said, "and see where we can go. Next week."

Soon it was Friday, and time for our party. Cynthia happened to phone me for some reason, so I invited her to come.

"Nini and Walter are here," I said. "You'll be able to see them." She had expressed fondness for Nini and Walter in the past.

"Who wants to see *them?*" Cynthia said.

"I thought you liked them."

"I don't want to see *them,*" Cynthia said.

"Don't you want to come to our party?"

"Well, it's a long ride. I'll see. Maybe it won't be so bad if I bring Cyril Bernstein. I'll have to let you know."

I decided that England had brought out the worst in Cynthia. I added her to a list of people I never wanted to see again. The list consisted so far of Mr. MacAllister, Mrs. Stackpole, Dr. Bott, the elephant lover at the zoo, Jane and her mother, and now Cynthia.

I walked across the street to Harrods and bought ham and chicken and some pastries. We counted out our scanty collection of mugs and cups, and Jordan rented some glasses from the pub on the comer.

Nini and Walter came early, followed by some normal-looking public relations people, and then Maud Tweak, towing a large man in tweeds.

"I hope you don't mind," she said, in a low, agitated voice. "My husband is here; I didn't expect him. Actually he's a guide in Switzerland, but he came home, so I brought him along."

We said we were delighted to meet Mr. Tweak, who seemed affable.

Basil Goldbrick, elegantly turned out and with a small white moustache, arrived with his wife Daisy, who was wearing a very large floppy hat and a lot of perfume. We served drinks to everyone, and they disposed themselves about the sitting room. Nini, who was a take-charge person, had pulled various throws and other swathings off a few armchairs. I had never unveiled these, assuming Mrs. Stackpole had swathed them because they were in an advanced state of dilapidation. Now I was surprised to see that they were new, or at least newly upholstered.

A lot of screeching drifted in from the street, and some theater people turned up, friends of the public relations guests. There was an actress with bangs touching her nose and a very short skirt. She looked to be about eighteen years old. The man who was with her got a drink and promptly fell through the seat of one of Mrs. Stackpole's antique chairs. "I'm terribly sorry," I said. We pulled him out, and he sat on a dining room chair and that broke. Needless to say, this occasioned a good deal of merriment.

We all sat down eventually and conversations ensued. "How have you been getting on?" Maud Tweak asked me, smiling all over her face.

I hesitated.

"I expect you'll get used to it," she said.

I took a deep breath, mindful of Jordan's having commented that I had said critical things during the dinner party at her apartment. "Look," I said carefully, "I'm afraid I gave you a false impression the other night. I don't want you to think I don't like it here... I'm afraid I must have sounded like the most awful malcontent."

"Oh, my dear," Maud Tweak said, glinting at me. Walter came over to us and settled himself for a chat.

"My goodness," he said, in his friendly, rather prissy way, "this is such a charming house."

"Yes, charming," Maud Tweak replied. "Really excellent taste. Of course, it's very expensive here. I'm afraid," she went on with no change of expression, "that you'll find a very different attitude among your people toward Vietnam when you get home."

"Will we," Walter said.

"Yes, I'm afraid so," Maud said. "I'm afraid world opinion is definitely against you."

"Is that an Angelica Kauffman I see on the wall?" Walter asked. He uncoiled his considerable length and drifted off.

"And those race riots," Maud Tweak said to me.

Jordan and I were completely out of touch with what was going on in the world. He had been immersed in English Pressclips, and I had spent months studying for my Master's exams. A few nights before, on TV, we had glimpsed what looked like American soldiers shooting at something in a jungle, and I had asked whether we were in some kind of war. Jordan wasn't sure about it.

"What's the race situation here?" I asked, to say something.

"It's most unfortunate," she responded promptly. "All these colored people coming here. Many of them don't even speak English."

"Yes, that's bad," I said. "At home blacks are part of American culture."

"Oh, come," Maud Tweak said in a shocked voice.

"I mean they speak English," I said defensively. "They're born there."

She continued to look at me, amused.

"When you say 'colored people'," I said, "you mean East Indians, don't you, and Pakistanis and Malaysians, as well as Africans."

"No, we don't," she said firmly.

"You don't? But in *A Passage to India*, for instance—"

"You've been reading a lot of books," she said accusingly. "None of it is true. One of my best friends is an Indian woman."

"I don't mean you personally. I mean the situation generally. What *is* the situation generally?"

"Well, it's certainly different from the States. I mean they can go to any hotel anywhere, and they aren't kept out, you know. They can eat anywhere. But," she said, "if for instance one should come here and want to rent this house, Mrs. Stackpole would not rent it to him, and quite rightly."

I stared at Maud Tweak, the good socialist.

"After all," she went on, possibly sensing my reaction, "this place has carpets and so on. You can't have people killing chickens in the corner and that sort of thing."

"But aren't any of them middle class? I mean educated ones, doctors. In America there's a black middle class…"

She glanced vaguely around the room. I noticed that her eyes were rather small and set close together.

"I suppose so," she said. "Some Embassy people perhaps."

This silenced me for a while. "I'd like to ask you something," I said finally. "We had a rather strange encounter at the theater the other night. There was this character with long hair—"

"Of course our men wear their hair longer than Americans. They prefer it that way."

"Yes, I know; I wasn't talking about that. I mean he had these sideburns, you know, side whiskers actually, and a sort of Edwardian get-up, a high collar and everything. I always associated that sort of thing with the Beatles, you know, Mods, rockers, sort of democratic people, protesting—"

"There's nothing to protest," she said stiffly.

"No, I mean the class thing," I said.

"There isn't any class thing in this country."

"There isn't any class thing in this country?"

"Of course not, there hasn't been for fifteen years."

That meant the class thing had suddenly keeled over in 1950.

"Well, anyway," I said, going on for some reason which escapes me now, "you see, this fellow in the theater with the sideburns and the collar, he was speaking in this strange affected drawl—"

"We say *you* drawl," Maud Tweak interjected swiftly. I had been intending to ask her if there was a Victorian Dandy movement afoot: snobbish Teddy boys or something, but I dropped it.

"Look," she said in a businesslike voice, "you come over here, asking a lot of questions, reading a lot of books. Nothing you think is true. It's all terribly out of date; you take me back fifteen years, you really do."

"But," I said, "there must be *something* to protest. There is, everywhere. How about the Royal Family? Doesn't anyone ever protest about *them?*"

"Of course not," Maud said, twitching restlessly. "No one."

"But the Beatles do," I said, conscious that our conversation had left logic far behind.

"They do not," she said.

"They do too," I replied, irritated. I considered myself an authority on the Beatles. "George Harrison said it."

"What did he say?"

"He said, 'Royalty is stupid.' You can't get a plainer statement than that."

"He didn't mean it."

"He did too mean it. Why would he say it if he didn't mean it? Aren't the Beatles a sign of something? Change?"

"The Beatles." She smiled indulgently. "Those boys aren't *intelligent*."

"Not...? But—"

"Oh, they're witty and all that. But they're not *intelligent*. They're just..." The phrase "working-class" hung in the air, beating its wings desperately. It didn't dare to light anywhere.

"Surely," I murmured, "there is discrimination based on accent?"

This stopped her cold for a minute.

"Look at the people in this room," she said finally. "None of them cares a fig for class."

I looked around at them. Daisy Goldbrick came from Liverpool and talked like Eliza Doolittle at a middle stage in her evolution; Manchester kept slipping in and out of her husband Basil's voice. The actress with the bangs spoke in a sort of die-away whisper. Maud's husband, who sounded forthrightly Yorkshire, was complaining bitterly about England. I felt myself irresistibly drawn to him.

"Our policemen are so dirty," he was announcing loudly. "Why do they have to wear those awful heavy dark dingy clothes? It's depressing to come here from France, their gendarmes are so *spruce...*"

It was time to descend into the basement and bring up food. Jordan and I took turns. I found it was impossible to hold the handrail while carrying a heavy tray up the steep winding staircase. A couple of times I had a bad off-balance moment: I saw myself ending here, a pathetic heap on the cheap linoleum, covered with imported ham and fragments of yellow-doodled china, dead, so to speak, among the alien corn. Luckily, I managed, barely, to regain my balance and toil upwards. It was very depressing after one emerged, white-faced and clammy from a brush with death, to find that someone needed a fork and have to pick one's way down again, carefully, with all that gin sloshing around inside one. Nobody offered to help us.

Everybody tucked into the food with good appetite. I sat down close to the actress, who, in addition to the skirt four inches above her knees, wore a bow over her bangs, long white stockings and flat Mary Jane shoes. The little of her face that was visible was heavily covered with eye makeup and white foundation. She looked even younger than at first impression—about fifteen years old. Maud had told me she was actually thirty-eight.

"What do you think of our television here?" she asked me in her faint, throaty voice.

"Oh, it's interesting. Of course it's only on for a limited time. And it rains so much, we could use more of it."

"But of course in the States, your children watch television so much that it's a health menace. Isn't it?"

"No, it isn't. They'd rather be outside in good weather. They don't watch it."

"No?" I had a feeling that her eyebrows were raised, although I couldn't see them. "We hear that it's a health menace in the States," she said firmly.

"I don't know why people in this country are so reluctant to try anything new," Hugh Tweak said, over his plate. "There's no initiative. They hate change; they want to do everything the way they always have."

"They are sort of rigid," I said cautiously.

"My God, yes," he said belting down some Scotch. "My God, they're rigid."

"I see you have a colored telephone," Maud Tweak said loudly to the company at large. "The telephone company is so helpful. They wake me every morning for work. I just leave a call, you know. The phone rings every morning at seven, and I pick up the receiver, and the operator says, 'Good morning, Mrs. Tweak, it's seven o'clock.' And I say, 'Good morning, what's the weather this morning?' And she says—"

I thought to myself that I could guess what the weather was like.

"You pay for that service," Hugh Tweak said, looking at his wife rather blearily.

"Only a token," she said.

"This morning," said Walter brightly, "we saw *such* an interesting thing, the Changing of the Guard." Walter was more than a bit of a wag. It was often impossible to tell when he was being serious.

"Oh yes, Buckingham Palace," Maud Tweak said. "They had to put the sentries inside the gates."

"Well, you know," Hugh said, "a sentry stepped on an American woman's foot."

Everyone laughed very hard at this except Jordan and Walter and me. Hugh sprang up and walked the length of the room, lifting his feet high and setting them down hard with every step.

"Right on her foot," he said. "American woman got very close to him, with her camera, you know, and he... brought his foot down..." He brought his own foot down sadistically. I winced.

"Embassies were alerted," Maud Tweak said, expiring with laughter.

"Notes were written," her husband said.

"Of course they must take their photographs," one of the public relations people said. "They'd be lost without cameras."

"I have an irresistible desire," Walter said, "to be photographed with the Archbishop of Canterbury, if he can be persuaded to put on his full regalia."

Jordan and Nini and I laughed first, then the other English people, with the exception of Maud Tweak, realized it was a joke, and joined in. Maud was looking in vain for an eye to catch; when she couldn't catch one, she realized belatedly that Walter was not serious and began to laugh very heartily.

Hugh Tweak wiped his eyes. "Stamped right on it," he murmured reminiscently.

The evening wore on. Daisy Goldbrick and Maud became involved in a cozy conversation in a corner. I looked surreptitiously at my watch; it was nearly one in the morning. At any minute they'll start to leave, I thought, and we can go to bed. My calf muscles and my shoulders were aching from my heavily laden treks up and down the stairs.

"I return to Switzerland tomorrow," Hugh said, while Jordan filled his glass again. I thought hopefully that he really ought to get some sleep. "I'm guiding a tour of Bell Telephone people round Switzerland."

"Yes, Americans," Maud said to Daisy. "A group of Americans."

Everybody began to flag except Maud and Hugh; Daisy and Basil were the first to leave. "Goodbye," Maud said to Daisy, with a hand-squeeze and an affectionate look. "I'll call you."

"Had you met Daisy before this?" I asked Maud, when they had left.

"Heavens, no," she said, rather disdainfully. "I never saw the woman before." She turned with some enthusiasm to Nini. "My dear," she said, "I should so much like to show you and your husband some sights."

Walter and Nini had been to London many, many times.

"That would be nice," Nini said.

"Do give me a ring tomorrow," Maud said, "and we'll set something up. I should like so much to see you again anyway, and I think I can show you a few things you aren't likely to see otherwise."

"What is it you do?" Hugh asked Walter, who replied that he taught English in a college. "Oh, that's interesting," Hugh said. "Tell me, is Shakespeare ever taught in schools in America?"

The next time I glanced at my watch, openly this time, I saw that it was nearly four o'clock. The conversation had dulled down considerably; they all looked tired except Maud Tweak, but no one seemed ready to go home. I knew that Nini and Walter wanted to stay to the last and talk about everybody, but why didn't the rest of them leave? Jordan shot me a look of despair. It was a Friday night, and he had been up since seven.

Finally, after another fifteen minutes or so, Walter gave up and rose to leave. All the others shot up with him. We babbled goodbye in the hall; Walter said something I didn't catch and everyone around him shouted with laughter. Maud Tweak clutched her husband's arm. "Oh, Hugh," she cried, "they're laughing at your umbrella!"

Actually, they were laughing at something else, but I thought it was rather interesting that she should have thought this. It seemed to me to reveal a somewhat defensive state of mind.

We finally crawled into bed at five a.m., more dead than alive.

I kept dreaming that Maud Tweak, with an enormous bouffant head, was trying to stamp on my foot. I was very restless and got up about ten with a splitting headache. The sky was overcast, everything looked gray. There were dirty dishes, full ashtrays and smudged cups and saucers everywhere.

28

The Portobello Road

WE ATE OUR USUAL BREAKFAST of delicious croissants and instant coffee, surrounded by debris. The street outside looked even gloomier and more gray than usual. About ten-thirty, the phone rang. It was Maud Tweak, sounding impatient. "Look," she said, "those friends of yours, the Watchucallits. Yes. Well, are they coming round today or not? They said something about wanting me to show them the city."

"I haven't heard from them," I croaked.

"We took them round last night after we left you," she said, "and showed them Fleet Street at night. I think they liked it; it's the sort of thing tourists love. In any case, I'm going to the hairdresser's; I shan't be back until about two. Have them call me, will you?"

I hung up and crept slowly down the stairs to the kitchen again. Jordan was just finishing his second cup of Nescafé.

"That was Maud Tweak," I said. "I hate her."

The phone rang again. After a moment I crept painfully back up the stairs. This time it was Nini.

"How are you?" she asked.

"I'm awful," I said."How are you?"

"We're fine. A little tired. You know your friend Maud Tweak drove us all around after we left you."

"How was it?"

"Well, it was boring because everything was shut. But why are you awful?"

"I'm tired."

"Oh?" she said, with a rising inflection. "Why?" She was a speech therapist with a strong interest in psychiatry. I knew her wheels were turning.

"Because I got to bed at five. Because there are dishes everywhere. It's raining...."

"Do you want us to help you with the dishes?"

"No, thanks. I'll manage. I've got to go now because Jordan is leaving. Oh—Maud Tweak will be at home after two this afternoon. She wants you to call her."

Jordan was now upstairs, combing his hair in the mildewed back bathroom with the hole in the ceiling. "I'll come back early and help you finish up," he said. "I must just get some stuff out of the way. I'm pretty sure Basil is going to buy in."

"He didn't say anything last night?"

"I could tell he was having a good time," Jordan said. "Anyway, if he doesn't buy in..."

The phone rang again, worsening my headache.

Suddenly we were very popular.

It was Walter this time. He sounded concerned. "Anita!" he cried. "Are you all right?"

"I have a headache."

"Well, Nini is worried. She said you sounded really desperate. We want you to let us hop in a cab and come over and do the dishes for you."

"I wouldn't dream of it."

"Nini is worried about you."

"All I have is a headache."

"Well, then, why don't you come out with us? We're going to the Portobello Road. Have you been there yet?"

"No," I said, sounding pathetic. "I mostly go to Harrods."

"Then you must come with us. Mark can look after the children." I decided to go and arranged to meet them there. I told Jordan I would be at his office by two o'clock.

It was raining in the Portobello Road on that Saturday morning. It was cold too, and dark, more like November than July. Stalls had been set up in the street and there were a good many people bartering and discussing antiques of all kinds. Most of them seemed to be late Victorian or more recent—the antiques, not the people. On every side we heard, "Now in dollars that would be…"

"It's fascinating here, isn't it?" Walter said. "So quaint." Appraising furniture, china and jewelry was his avocation; his father had had an antiques shop.

"Ur," I said, vaguely. My head still ached; I was cold and depressed.

"They expect you to bargain," Nini said. She stopped at a stall and picked up a broken doll with staring china eyes. "How much?" she said, to a tall youth with one gold earring and a sort of sheepskin slung over his shoulder.

"Two pounds."

"That's ridiculous," Nini said. "It's not worth it."

"Make an offer," the youth said reasonably.

"What do you want it for?" I asked.

"Seven shillings," Nini said. The youth smiled sarcastically.

"It's broken anyway," Nini said.

We drifted away into a shop with rugs.

"Oh, look," I said, trying to perk up a little, "Oriental rugs." I pointed at one.

"I'll get it for you," Nini said, and darted away.

"I don't want it," I said to Walter, who shrugged.

Nini became involved in a heated discussion with a fat man at the rear of the shop. He *looked* Victorian: I expected to see a pile of bones and rags in a corner. She darted back."I can get that for you for sixty dollars," she said, pointing to a large torn item. "It's a steal."

"How would I get it back in the plane?" I asked nastily. "Carry it on my head? Anyway I haven't got sixty dollars. Anyway I don't want it."

The fat man came near, hovering. "Well?" he said, as we left.

"Too much money," Nini snapped at him.

We began to walk through the outdoor stalls again. Walter picked up a horn glass, one of a set of six, all cracked.

"My goodness," he said. "Horn glasses."

"What would you do with them?" I asked. I had decided to be difficult. I felt like it.

"Well, you see," he explained, "they're made out of horn. That's interesting. Of course," he added regretfully, "they're chipped somewhat."

"Would you *drink* out of them?" I asked. The sky was very dark and low; drifts of water blew across our faces.

"My goodness," Walter said. He set them down gently.

A moment later Nini cried out in delight. She had come upon a green velvet bellows; it was small and heart-shaped. The velvet was faded and rotting in spots. When she squeezed it a weak puff of dust wheezed out.

"It's charming," Nini said.

All down the street, people were pawing over these broken remains. We heard music and looked up: a very small, fragile old man was pushing a wicker baby carriage down the sidewalk, or pavement. He was wearing a sort of nineteenth-century ball costume: a black stovepipe hat, a long, swallow-tailed black coat, very narrow black trousers and little black pumps on his tiny feet. An ancient gramophone, perched on the foot of the baby carriage, was grinding out a dim tune. In the carriage, with only his head protruding from a tattered blanket, was a small brown and white dog.

"Oh, Walter!" Nini cried. "If only we had our camera!"

"Oh, we forgot it," Walter said.

"That's always the way," I said, looking at my watch. "Gracious, it's after one. I told Jordan I'd meet him at the office."

"But you don't want to leave now," Nini said. "We haven't seen anything yet."

I could spot another baby carriage coming toward us: this one was being pushed by a hugely fat woman and was emitting scratchy music; I could hear it already. I made my escape and arrived at Jordan's office, where I found the children, without shoes. They had gone out into the street to look at something, and Eric had shut the door, which locked behind them. So they had taken a cab to the office. We all took another cab back to Baldridge Place, where the older boys leaped over puddles in their socks, and Jordan carried Eric into the house. He didn't weigh much.

We cleaned up the rest of the mess and then sat drearily watching television while the rain dribbled outside, and no one came down the street. Every Saturday afternoon half of a movie was shown on the TV, usually a Western. Today, the announcer said, it was "Barbara Stennick in *Kettle Queen of Colorado*."

29

At the Bilkingtons'

THE FOLLOWING SUNDAY, we were scheduled to take a train to the countryside again to be entertained by the citizenry. This time it was Dampton, Bucks, to spend the afternoon with the Bilkingtons, friends of the Foyles. The houses in Dampton were larger than those in Cramley where Rose Emily lived, although constructed, like Rose Emily's, of orange brick and set on narrow lots, each house the same distance from the street. The Bilkingtons had three children: a girl, Stephanie, who was Mark's age, and two little boys, Rodney and William.

Mrs. Bilkington met us at the door; she was attired in smart tweeds. I had used my head for once and was wearing what in Chicago we always referred to as "a fall suit."

"I see you know what to wear," Mrs. Bilkington said approvingly.

The house was much bigger than poor Rose Emily's. We stepped into a spacious entrance hall, decorated with a large framed photograph of the Queen in voluminous blue robes, walking somewhat in advance of the Duke of Edinburgh, similarly robed. She was glancing at him over her shoulder, evidently saying something and looking rather annoyed.

"We took that photograph last month," Mrs. Bilkington said. "You can see we were very close to her." The Bilkingtons drove us about the area, showing us William Penn's tomb, which we were surprised to find was in England, and people playing cricket.

"It's a boring game," Mr. Bilkington said sadly. "They just stand around in those white clothes and then change positions every time someone hits the ball. There's really nothing to see."

After that we all went back to the house for tea: little sandwiches and tea with milk, and then little cakes and tea with milk. I had discovered to my disappointment that taking tea at four or five o'clock, a custom that I had always admired as particularly civilized when I read about it or saw it in English movies, made me feel odd and spoiled my appetite for dinner at eight, or even ten, or in fact at any hour. The Bilkingtons poured a lot of sugar in their tea and spread jam on everything. I had a considerable sweet tooth myself, and had noted with approval the many appealing candy bar commercials on television in the late evening, and the fact that candy and cakes were sold in the legitimate theaters.

On our previous trip to England as tourists, we sat at the theater in front of a couple who ordered pastry during the intermission, or interval. This couple, a man and woman in their middle fifties, shared their plate of cakes with a rapture that we found charming. "Oh ooh," the lady cried, "oh, halve this one, it's *too* good!" "Oh yes," her companion cried, "but do halve this one—look, it's full of cream!" "Oh, it's so terribly good," she responded, "oh, do halve this one, mind the chocolate." "Ooh, mm," he said.

We were entranced with this little episode, and afterward told each other and anyone else who would listen, that it demonstrated the impressive ability of the English to derive enjoyment from the simplest things in life: English men, in particular, since we could not imagine an American male gasping and cooing over a plate of cakes. 'They *enjoy* things," we said. "They know how to draw the last drop of pleasure from their experiences."

I thought of this as we shared tea with the Bilkington family. Stephanie Bilkington was fifteen, Mark's age. She was a shy, slender, very pretty child in a severe suit and heavy brown oxfords. Her hair was parted on the side; she wore it the way Princess Elizabeth had worn her hair at the age of ten, and tried unsuccessfully to hide behind it.

"Oh, Mummy," she said, "today the Geography Mistress was talking about the yacht *Brittania*. One of the girls said it was expensive to run it just to take the Queen to Scotland. The mistress said it wasn't such a great expense; after all, it is the Queen."

Mrs. Bilkington set her cup down with a majestic gesture and turned partway in her chair to face Stephanie, who tried to shrink back behind her hair.

"What your mistress should have told you," Mrs. Bilkington said, addressing us all, "what your Geography Mistress should have told you, Stephanie, is that the *Brittania* is a hospital ship. It must be maintained in any case because it is a hospital ship, vital in time of war. The Queen's taking it to Scotland is incidental; it costs nothing extra."

"Oh, Mummy," Stephanie said faintly, "I wish I'd known."

"You should have known," Mrs. Bilkington said kindly, "but you may tell your little friend."

"Oh, thank you, Mummy," Stephanie said.

"I have a friend," Mrs. Bilkington said to us, "who travelled with the Queen and the Duke at one time on their ship. She travelled with them on the same ship. She told me that Philip likes to call her Betty." She paused. "Yes," she said," he calls her Betty. I know it's true because I happened to be sitting quite near them at a polo match and I heard him call her Betty. I think he said, 'Oh, Betty, hand me my sweater,' or something like that."

"Oh, Mummy," Stephanie said.

Rodney and William sat side by side in little gray wool shorts with matching jackets. Rodney was nine, only a year younger than Bruce, but about half his size. He had enormous frightened eyes in a thin face; his little legs stuck out of his shorts like matchsticks. William, six, was also rather under-sized, but he had a rosy complexion and seemed fairly outgoing. "It's time for *Stingray*," he said.

"Oh, *Stingray*," Mr. Bilkington said. He had been quietly dozing on a fat red sofa that matched the two fat red armchairs. "Oh, I never miss *Stingray*." He looked at his wife. "I suppose it's all right if I just watch it," he said.

"Yes, go along," she said indulgently. "Rodney," Rodney shot up, a look of terror on his face. "Just take your guests into the playroom," his mother told him. He herded Eric and Bruce off with him and Mr. Bilkington and William.

"*I* don't like it," Stephanie said. "It's all fighting, you know. For boys."

"I don't know what to do about Rodney," Mrs. Bilkington said. "He seems rather unsure of himself."

"He seems shy," Jordan said.

"Well, he is rather shy. So we are going to try sending him off to boarding school in the autumn. Perhaps that will bring him out of himself."

"Oh, Rodney's awful," Stephanie said, giggling and looking at Mark from behind her hair. "He teases me."

"I've spoken to the doctor about it," Mrs. Bilkington went on, "but there doesn't seem to be a detectable reason for his hesitant attitude."

"Oh, Doctor Killman," Stephanie said shyly.

"Stephanie loves Doctor Killman," Mrs. Bilkington explained. "He's our doctor."

"We could use a good doctor," Jordan said, obviously thinking of Dr. Bott. "We don't have one at the moment."

"Oh, Doctor Killman is excellent," Mrs. Bilkington said. "We have used him for years, he couldn't be better. Of course," she added, "he's Jewish." She paused a moment to let that sink in. "Now I realize," she went on, "that many people will not use a Jewish doctor because they feel he will refer them to other Jewish doctors if they need special treatment or anything of that kind. We were hesitant ourselves about it. But I may say with confidence that Doctor Killman will not recommend another doctor unless it's necessary and not unless he is a good one, Jewish or otherwise."

"That's good," Jordan said.

"Yes, many people hesitate to use Jewish doctors," Mrs. Bilkington said.

"I love Doctor Killman," Stephanie remarked.

"I'll give you his name," Mrs. Bilkington said to Jordan. "You can feel absolutely confident about him."

"I wish you could come up with something for the children to do every day," I said, whining as usual. "We have an awful time, especially in bad weather."

"Children love Madame Tussaud's," she said. "Have you taken them there?"

"Well, actually," I said, "Eric was frightened to death by it. He was frightened of the Hamlet diorama, and he was terrified of the Queen Mother."

"The Queen Mum!"

"Yes, it's weird, isn't it? The thing's got a funny look in its eyes."

"Frightened of the Queen Mum!" Mrs. Bilkington couldn't get over it. "That's really amusing, you know, and the Queen Mum would be the first to laugh at it, because she has an absolutely marvelous sense of humor. And she has a twinkle in her eye. I suppose they tried to catch that in the wax figure...."

"It sort of leers," I said.

"Yes, they tried to catch that twinkle. Everyone knows, you see, that the Queen Mum has a twinkle in her eye. She's known for it. She goes about everywhere, you see, and everyone loves to see her, because she cheers them up. She's such a happy person. And she would laugh at Eric, you know, because she's the first to get a joke. Everyone always says that. Actually, I've seen her, and she really is a very jolly person. She really does have a twinkle in her eye." Mrs. Bilkington laughed reminiscently. "The Queen Mum," she said, subsiding.

I didn't have to look at Jordan, who sat beside me in a wing chair; I could tell from his gentle breathing that he was asleep.

"Speaking of the Royal Family," Mrs. Bilkington said.

"I and my husband," Stephanie remarked, laughing. Mark looked at her.

"Yes," Mrs. Bilkington said, "she always used to say, 'I and my husband' and of course her voice is rather high. Now she's changed it a little to avoid being laughed at. She says, 'My husband and I.'"

"I and my husband," Stephanie said, in a high voice.

"Now she says, 'My husband and I.' She tries to vary it," Mrs. Bilkington explained. "Speaking of the Royal Family, I must just show you the rest of the photographs I took last month. I was standing quite close to everything, I had a wonderful place, really. I wrote away for it a year ago."

She rose and went to rummage in a drawer.

"What do you think of the Beatles?" Mark asked Stephanie, tensely.

"Oh, I really prefer Bing Crosby," Stephanie replied. "Don't you?"

"Here they are," Mrs. Bilkington said. "Now here's the first. His name probably won't mean anything to you, but this man is the Queen's Secretary. I caught him standing in this window, he was right above us. I just happened to look up."

"My goodness," I said loudly, clearing my throat. "Look at this." I handed the photograph to Jordan, poking him with my elbow to wake him up. Mrs. Bilkington had taken quite a lot of photographs. I looked at them and passed them to Jordan who looked at them and passed them on to Mark.

"Ha ha," Mark said. "The Queen looks funny in this blue bathrobe."

My heart missed a beat. There was a frozen silence before Mrs. Bilkington spoke calmly. "Those are official robes actually," she said. "It's traditional to wear them."

The boys and Mr. Bilkington came back from viewing *Stingray.*

"It was awfully good this time," Mr. Bilkington said. "They were trapped on a forbidden planet."

Eventually we thanked the Bilkingtons for their hospitality, and straggled back to the station. We explained to Mark at some length that he shouldn't have laughed at the Queen. After a while the train came, and we boarded, stuffed with sweets, tired and very crabby. We arrived at Marylebone Station in a sullen silence and emerged into the eerie stillness of the Sunday London streets. We couldn't even think of dinner until well after ten o'clock.

30

Afternoon at Margaret's

MARGARET LEECH had invited us to spend Sunday afternoon at her apartment so that Bruce and Eric could play with her son Michael. We felt sympathetic toward Michael because of the pleasure everyone seemed to take in his humiliation after he called a passerby a twit, and because of his projected banishment to an English boarding school: an institution which my reading on the subject led me to consider as a cross between an army camp and a federal penitentiary, with a lot of Latin thrown in.

We took a cab through the deadly silent streets. Nothing stirred, not even a cat. "At least we don't have to take a train," Jordan said. When we got out of the cab, we encountered Maud Tweak, slim in very tight Levis and a silk pink blouse, carrying a string bag filled with goodies. She scooped us up and led us upstairs to the flat. Michael, a smallish child with big dark eyes, was waiting in the hall. He threw his arms around Eric's neck and they went off chummily to an inner room, Bruce and Mark trailing.

The roomy flat had matching Swedish modern furniture and wallpaper with ivy and trellises on it. There was a large window offering a view of the gloomy gray Sunday sky. Margaret served us wine—apparently tea was considered to be middle class or something by whatever caste Maud Tweak and

Margaret Leech belonged to. They turned their noses up at the very mention of the stuff.

"I'm glad you wore slacks," Maud said, glancing at my blue madras pants. 'They're regulation Sunday attire around here." Again I had fortunately chosen the correct uniform, although madras may have been a little over the edge. My conformist American instincts might have been in play here. The British press wrote a lot about American conformism.

"You'll like the people who are coming today," Maud Tweak said to us. 'They're Jewish." She went on, after a pause, her eyes snapping with malice. "Such an interesting party you had the other night. Who *was* that fascinating woman in the floppy green hat?"

"Daisy Goldbrick," I said. "You seemed so friendly, I thought you had met her before."

"Never laid eyes on the woman. But she *did* fasten onto me, didn't she?"

The doorbell rang, and Albert entered, dressed sportily and reeking of garlic as usual. "I was just talking about the Millers' party," Maud told him. "Such interesting people. And of course I took the What's-Their-Name around afterward. I showed them Fleet Street at night. I think they loved it."

"Are your friends American?" Albert asked politely.

"He is," I said, but Nini's—"

"Dutch-French," Maud said. "With a strong dash of American."

"I liked your husband," I said to Maud.

"Oh, did you? Yes, I daresay he seems very nice on first meeting."

The doorbell rang again, and a very fat blonde woman with an enormous nose came in, and lay down full length on the floor. She was wearing slacks too, and carrying a velvet handbag. "Don't say a word," she said. "I have to do this for my back. It's the only way it's comfortable."

"Poor dear," Maud said. "Your poor back. Have you had an awful time?"

"I threw her out," the woman said. "I told her to get out."

"Her *au pair* girl," Margaret said to me. "I have one too. You know, they come here to learn English. Usually from Italy. They're all impossible."

"Threw her out," the fat woman said.

"This is Anastasia Silverman," Margaret said. We all murmured how do you do. Margaret asked her, "What happened to Gregory?"

"He had to go out," she responded cryptically. "But I brought George."

A small blond boy darted around the room with Michael in hot pursuit. I assumed this was George.

"I'm interested that you liked Hugh," Maud Tweak said to me. "So many people do when they first meet him. Of course he's very charming to strangers. But you know he didn't say a word to me all the way home."

"Is that so," I said.

Mark came into the room. "They're killing Bruce and Eric," he remarked.

Nobody moved, except me. I rose and followed Mark down the hall to a small bedroom where Michael and George were wrestling on an enormous bed. Bruce and Eric were standing in a corner, staring at them. "You'd better be careful," I said, to Michael and George.

George reached down on the floor and picked up a shoe. He threw it and hit Mark in the head.

"Hey! "Mark said.

Michael laughed hoarsely. "Good for you," he said. He slid off the bed and lunged at Eric, who slipped behind Bruce. Michael kicked Bruce in the shins. "Ow," Bruce said. George laughed and jumped on Michael's back. They began to roll over the floor, kicking out very hard at everyone. "Listen here," I said.

"What's the matter with these brats?" Mark asked.

"I think they're both disturbed," Bruce observed. "They've got problems."

"Let's go home," Eric said.

This was a sensible suggestion, but instead I went into the living room and said brightly, "My goodness, they certainly are lively children. I'm afraid my kids can't cope with them."

Anastasia, who was now sitting on the Swedish modem sofa, stared at me coldly.

"They seem to be fighting," I said, sitting down on the matching chair.

"Boys always fight," Maud Tweak said. "I helped with Michael's birthday party. They were rolling all over the floors. Breaking things. I was simply exhausted."

Everybody smiled indulgently, except Jordan and me.

"Yes, everybody likes Hugh when they first meet him," Maud Tweak said, "but you don't know of course what I've had to put up with. I mean here is this man with a successful position in advertising, and suddenly he announces that he can't work anymore. He had been seeing this psychiatrist, you see, and of course that did it, you know. I mean he had to stay home for a year and *find* himself. There was absolutely no money coming in so I said, 'Look', you know, 'this won't do'. So he went off to be a guide in Switzerland and Spain and I found my job and now of course it's better. But I mean, my dear, listening to him. Telling me for hours how impossible I am, how plain I am."

"That's very destructive," I said.

"Oh, my dear, it's most destructive. And then at one point he wanted me to go off and live on a mountaintop in the Basque country so he could write." She laughed heartily. "I said, Look, my dear, you've got the wrong person for that, you know."

"I love the Basque country," Anastasia said. "I've been there many times."

"I went to see his psychiatrist," Maud went on. "He lived in Swiss Cottage. Of course," she said significantly, "they all do. And I mean I simply could not get through to the man. Finally I said, 'Look', you know, 'this won't do at all, just give me a drink and I'll go'. And I went."

"My goodness," I said.

"They're impossible," Maud said. "Psychiatrists."

"You have a lot of them, don't you?" Margaret said to me. "In the United States."

"Well, we have them. We're psychologically oriented."

"Yes, you certainly are," Maud said. "I hope your friends had a good time. We drove them all round Fleet Street last night, the sort of thing tourists love. And we sent them to the theater. Noel Coward." She looked at me expectantly.

"My goodness," I said.

"Yes, Noel Coward." She added cryptically, "I thought that would be suitable. They insisted on taking me to dinner. First we went to a pub, Saturday. They had beer, of course. I didn't bother with all that nonsense, I drank whiskey."

She and Margaret laughed heartily. "And what an interesting party you had," Maud said. "I was wild about that woman in the floppy hat."

"Is she American?" Margaret asked. She turned to me with a smile. "We always laugh at American women and their funny hats."

"No," I said, "she's English."

"Are you going to travel from here?" Anastasia asked me. "Are you going to the Continent?"

"Oh, no," I said. "We can't afford it." Something like a film slid over her rather prominent pale eyes; the corner of her mouth turned down, permanently. "Oh," she said frigidly.

I babbled about the business, while Maud went on talking to Margaret.

"... exhausted, and then that awful evening," she was saying. "And then the next day that silly ass Walter..."

Mark came into the room and sat disconsolately on a plastic hassock in front of the fireplace. I sipped wine. Suddenly Anastasia's son rocketed into the room, followed closely by Michael. Both of them leapt on Mark: one clutched him around the neck, kneeling on his lap, while the other seized him from behind, crawling up his back. Mark reacted violently; one of the little tykes fell back against me. The wine spurted everywhere.

"Be careful!" Anastasia snapped at Mark.

"My goodness, Mark," I said. People began rushing around looking for damp cloths. Maud took my handbag, a natty burlap number, and carefully scrubbed at it. "Here," she said humbly, handing it back. "I did the best I could. I hope it's all right."

"It's fine," I said. "Forget it."

Bruce and Eric were discovered standing behind me, looking even more disconsolate than Mark, who now stood by the window, watching the gray rain.

"One hit me on the head twice," Bruce said. "And the other one kicked Eric. They hit each other, and then they broke a perfume bottle."

"I want to go home," Eric said.

"Gracious," I said to Anastasia."I hope we never go to war with you. You'd knock us silly." She didn't seem to think that was funny. I knew perfectly well that if we went to war with them, *we'd* knock *them* silly. I was trying ineptly to suggest that our children were quiet, peace-loving citizens, while theirs were obviously sociopaths of some kind, and I was hoping she would try to get her kid to cool it. But she didn't.

Margaret and Maud brought out trays with crackers on them, containing dabs of various kinds. While we consumed the crackers, Anastasia kept eyeing Mark with noticeable distaste.

"Now that you've eaten," I said to Bruce lightheartedly, "you can hit the road."

Maud gave a shriek of laughter. "Yes, that's good," she said. "They can understand *that,* that's the sort of language they understand. Hit the road," she said to Eric, who was sucking his thumb in an agony of bleary boredom.

The English newspaper columnists insisted constantly that American children did not know how to behave, that they were wild and undisciplined. While at the same time Americans were dull conformists.

"Michael is going off to boarding school in the autumn," Anastasia said to me. "That will improve him considerably."

I said that I hoped so.

After we had all settled into our seats once again, with our two children wandering miserably in and out and Mark huddled by the fireplace, there was a pause, which Jordan rushed to fill: "Boy," he said, "did we ever see something horrible on television last night. Have you ever heard of someone called Spike Milligan?"

Something told me he shouldn't have phrased the question in quite that way.

"Oh, Spike Milligan, of course," Maud Tweak said. "So terribly funny. Charming, really."

"We love Spike Milligan," Margaret Leech said.

Spike Milligan mumbled a lot and ran around, acting out jokes. Sometimes he wore a pith helmet and sometimes he wore a fright wig. Sometimes someone would pull out a drawer and find him in it. Some of his jokes were obscene and some were satirical on the level of *Mad* magazine. Since his TV show recurred with depressing regularity, I assumed he must have a following of some kind.

"You needn't feel bad about not liking him," Maud Tweak said generously. "I mean it isn't because you're a foreigner or anything. Some *English* people don't care for him."

"I can well believe it," I said.

"He is one of our great British eccentrics," Anastasia said, fixing me with a pale cold eye. Margaret and Maud began to regale each other with memorable moments from "The Spike Milligan Show."

"And the time he ate the frog…"

"And the time he kicked the ball of yarn and it was really a stone…"

I looked furtively at my watch. It was after four. But I didn't know whether we could leave yet. The rain continued to drizzle down the window. They had gone to some trouble, putting the dabs on the crackers and opening the wine bottle.

"How are you enjoying London?" Anastasia said to me.

"Oh, I'm finding it difficult to entertain the children," I said, airing my obsession.

"You must take them to Battersea," she said. "It's ever so much nicer than Coney Island."

"I don't know anything about Coney Island," I said, with some hauteur. "And of course it's been so cool. And wet."

"Yes," she said, grudgingly. "The weather has been bad."

"I mean it's odd to think," I went on, "that it's been ninety degrees at home all week. Normally, of course, I don't like that kind of heat, but—"

"That's too hot," Anastasia said.

"Oh, yes, it's too hot, I know. But you see then it cools off, and the contrast—"

"That's too hot."

"Yes, but you see the contrast… It's—"

"Much," Anastasia said finally, "too hot."

I subsided and tried to think of something nice to say. "I do love the fruits and vegetables," I said. "And the bread. Our bread at home is awful, packaged bread, I mean. But even your sliced bread—"

"I never buy sliced bread," Anastasia said.

"I wouldn't dream of it," Maud put in.

"Oh, no," I said, "but I mean that even your packaged bread—"

"I never buy bread packaged," Margaret said.

The door opened and a girl with wild black hair and bedroom slippers appeared on the threshold. "Did you need me?" she asked. "I've been on the phone." It was the *au pair* girl. Eric slipped into the room again under her arm and stood behind the sofa, sucking his thumb. "I want to go home," he said.

"In a minute, dear," I replied. Jordan looked at me helplessly.

The girl went out. "They're beasts, all of them," Anastasia said to Margaret. "When Michael is at school you can let her go."

I had no desire to discuss the private school concept—or anything else—with her, but she apparently wanted to discuss it with me. Or to talk to me about it: Anastasia seemed to prefer to make pronouncements, rather than to engage in discussions.

"Any child," she said, "who whines about his life at private school should be ignored."

"Somerset Maugham?" I asked humbly.

"Sheer exhibitionism," she snapped.

"Did *you* go to public school?"

"No, but my brother did."

"And how did he like it?"

"Well, my mother took him out. He hated it and it was making him ill. I mean," she elaborated, apparently sensing an inconsistency in her remarks, "we couldn't allow him to become ill. The doctor," she added, producing a trump card, "the doctor told my mother to send him to day school."

Michael and his little friend reappeared. It was time for *Stingray*, the adventure story with rubber puppets in outer space which the boys had been exposed to in Dampton, Bucks. Here the TV set was in the living room and we were all going to watch *Stingray* together. Since the British producers intended the show to appeal to the American market, all the sympathetic characters spoke with strong Midwestern American accents.

"Look at that square-jawed American face," Maud Tweak said, gesturing at the screen. It wasn't American, it wasn't even a real face, but it fit her world view.

Anastasia began to tell me all about her projected holiday. "A little beach," she said, "and the small hotel…"

It sounded really attractive. Jordan seemed to think it did too. He glanced at me and nodded significantly.

"Let's go home!" Eric cried out suddenly. "I'm sick of this place!"

He had been tried beyond endurance. We all had, if the truth be known.

"How rude," Anastasia breathed at him.

"Don't be rude, dear," I said automatically, and hypocritically. We called a cab and it didn't come, and it didn't come. Finally we decided to go downstairs and wait for it in the street; we couldn't bear the flat any longer. Jordan and the boys went out into the hall. I suddenly remembered that I had not said goodbye to Anastasia, who had been out of the room when we bade farewell to Margaret and Maud Tweak. I went back to the living room and discovered Anastasia and Maud dancing arm in arm in obvious relief at our departure.

"Goodbye, Anastasia," I said.

They both stopped and quickly separated. "Goodbye," Anastasia said.

When we got home, I told Jordan I had decided I was not going to pay any more Sunday afternoon visits.

"I'm with you," he said. "But Daisy Goldbrick wants us to come out and see her garden."

"I don't think Eric will enjoy Daisy Goldbrick's garden. I'm finished. I'm disillusioned and tired. What's more, I'm hostile."

"I can see that," he said sadly.

"Aren't you?" I asked.

"We need a vacation," he said, changing the subject. "Some place... a small hotel, a little beach... some place where the sun is always shining."

The next day we went down to the American Express office to book a flight somewhere, anywhere, warm. Every place warm was filled up. No flights to Spain, France or Italy. In desperation we asked about Ireland. Ireland was filled up too. The truth was that we could not get onto a plane leaving England for happier climes; everybody else had beaten us to it.

"How about Devon?" Jordan asked, remembering Cynthia's friend Althea Bradgood.

"She told us to motor through Devon and Cornwall," I said.

"Oh, yes," the American Express man said. "The English Riviera."

"Motor?" Jordan said. "Are you crazy? Drive on English roads with all those English drivers coming at you?"

"Torquay," the man said.

"What?" Jordan said.

"Torquay," the man repeated. "On the English Riviera. The largest town, definitely best for your purposes."

"Is it warm there?"

"Oh, yes, it's always warm in Devon, you know. The Castle Hotel. A five star hotel."

We left the place happy. In a couple of weeks we were going away, away from Baldridge Place with the basement kitchen and the mold from the gray rainy street and the gloomy pile of Harrods warehouse at the end of it. We were going to stay at a five star hotel on the English Riviera, a stone's throw from the beach, where it was always warm. Hurrah! we cried, and threw our caps in the air.

31

The Green Line

JORDAN'S LAWYER Percy Snell phoned and said that Mrs. Stackpole had informed him that she wished to inspect the house, to see for herself the damage done by the flood.

"It's already been inspected," I said.

"It's her right to see it," Jordan said reasonably. "Percy Snell said so."

"Percy Snell is an idiot," I said. "I talked to him on the phone and I could tell."

"The fact that Percy Snell is an idiot," Jordan said, in measured tones, "is beside the point. The law is on her side. She's coming on the twelfth."

"That's the day we're leaving."

"Percy Snell will take her around the house. We won't have to see her."

Mrs. Grail, too, had heard from our landlady. "Ah, the cheek of the creature," she said. "I've had another note from her and I've burned it. Ah, they think they own the world. And today someone called and asked to speak to me, and I said, 'Who is it calling please?' and she said, very nasty, 'What difference does it make to you? I want to speak to Mrs. Grail.' And I said, 'This is Mrs. Grail speaking,' and she said, 'Oh, Mrs. Grail, I'm sorry, but I didn't know it was you.'"

"She thought it was me. I," I said, stung but still grammatical.

"Ah, the cheek of them. So she said, 'Mrs. Stackpole would like you to call her or can she come to see you,' and I said, 'I work nights and I have no time.' And I hung up on her, the cheeky thing. Of course it's a lie about working nights, but I won't see her, and I'll never see her, the snip. And I'll tell you another thing," she said, dropping her voice. "She's never gone to Scotland at all, and she's been here in Knightsbridge the whole time, watching us. I saw her the other day."

When Sunday rolled around again, we congratulated ourselves. "We don't have to go visiting anymore," we said to each other. "The whole day is at our disposal." The sun was shining fitfully; it was cool but not cold.

"Today could we take a sightseeing bus?" Eric asked. He had noticed sightseeing buses driving about London and I had promised him that one day we would go on a sightseeing bus tour.

"Yes," Jordan said. "We have the whole day to ourselves and today we will take a sightseeing bus."

We took a cab to the bus depot and found a line of people waiting to mount a line of buses.

"Where does this bus go?" Jordan asked the elderly uniformed attendant. The elderly attendant ignored Jordan.

"Where does this bus go?" Jordan asked again, still pleasantly.

"Why doesn't he *answer* you?" I asked, enraged.

"Never mind," Jordan said. "Let's get into line."

As we stood in line, I reminded Jordan of the elderly movie theater attendant who had snubbed him, the elderly attendant in the supermarket who had jerked her chin wordlessly at the next aisle when I asked her where the bread was, the uniformed attendant at the Tower of London who had barked at a compatriot of ours for taking pictures of the front gate at a distance of some twenty feet.

"Calm down," Jordan said.

I mentioned the uniformed individual who, just after Jordan and Mark and two adults had disembarked, had slammed the door of the Underground train, narrowly missing Eric and Bruce and me. We were trapped on the train, huddled against the doors along with two little frightened girls, whose frustrated parents stood outside beating against the glass, while Jordan tried with superhuman effort to pry the doors open again. He kept shouting at the attendant to open the doors, and the attendant kept shouting at him to get away from the doors. Jordan stepped back from the doors, and the train sped away. At the next stop, I shepherded the little girls and my sons onto a train going back. The little girls had tried to get on another train going forward, an action which would have separated them from their parents indefinitely, or possibly forever.

"Calm down," Jordan repeated.

"I'll never calm down," I said. "I'll never be the same again."

The attendant came by and thrust a pamphlet into Jordan's hand.

"This bus passes Harrods and Buckingham Palace and St Paul's and the Houses of Parliament," Jordan said.

We've seen them all already," I said.

"We've seen them a thousand times," Bruce said.

"I want to take a sightseeing bus," Eric said. "You said we could take a sightseeing bus."

"I said we could take a sightseeing bus," Jordan told him, "but this sightseeing bus takes us to see sights we've already seen."

"You've seen Buckingham Palace," Bruce said.

"I want to see the sights," Eric said. "You said we could."

Several people turned and looked at us.

"You've already seen them," I said, in a low voice. "Why should we spend money to see things we've seen?"

"Don't argue with him," Mark said loudly. Everybody turned and looked at us.

"Be quiet," Jordan said.

"Oh, this is very embarrassing," I said.

"I want to see the sights," Eric said. He began to cry, very loudly.

There was another bus depot across the street.

"We'll take another sightseeing bus," Jordan said.

Eric was crying too loudly to hear him.

"Stop crying," Mark said.

Eric continued to cry.

"We'll take," I said, "Eric…"

We had attracted considerable attention. Jordan seized Eric's hand and dragged him off; a long wail trailed after them. Bruce and I followed, and Mark sauntered behind us, trying to pretend that he didn't know us. In the bus depot across the street, Jordan attempted to communicate with Eric.

"Stop… crying," he said slowly.

"Want… see…"

"We'll take a Green Line bus," Jordan said. "These are sightseeing buses."

Eric caught his breath. "Okay," he said finally.

"See, it says 'Tours'," Bruce said.

"I don't know why he always has to have his own way," Mark said.

Jordan went up to a young man at a counter, and asked him what tour he would suggest. The young man hesitated. "There's a nice one to Hindhead," he said. Jordan turned to us. I was giving Eric a tissue so he could blow his nose.

"He says there's a nice one to Hindhead," Jordan said.

"Is that better than the one marked 'Thames Valley'?" I asked.

"She wants to know if that's better than the one called 'Lower Thames Valley.'" Jordan said.

"Oh, they're all nice," the young man said.

"What's in Hindhead?" Jordan asked him.

"Oh, it's on the road to Portsmouth," the man answered. "It's on the Portsmouth road."

"How long does it take?"

"Five hours."

We all turned to Eric. "Now it's a five hour tour," Jordan said severely. "Two and a half hours going and two and a half hours coming back, do you understand?"

"Yes," Eric said.

"Now are you willing to sit still all that time? And will you be quiet?"

"Yes," Eric said, sniffing.

"If you start to complain, I'll bust you one," Mark said.

"That isn't necessary," I said to Mark.

"We'll take five tickets," Jordan said to the man. "What did you say was in Hindhead?" The man had his head down, counting the tickets.

"What did he say?" I asked Jordan.

"I think he said something about a cathedral." We walked slowly to the big green bus. "Five hours is a long time, Eric," Bruce said. "I hope you understand."

"My goodness, that was cheap," Jordan said cheerfully. "Very reasonable."

We climbed aboard. "Something tells me not to do this," I said.

The other people already seated were on the whole rather old, and some had missing teeth. "We can still back out," Jordan said. "What do you think, Eric?"

"I want to sit next to the window," Eric said. There were plenty of seats. Jordan told him to sit by himself next to the window.

"Remember this was your idea," Mark said to Eric.

"I hope you understand the situation," Bruce said to Eric.

We waited about fifteen minutes, and then the bus pulled out.

We drove and drove. It began to rain.

"Everybody on this bus is English," I said.

The old people waved and called to cars as they went by.

"What did he say was in Hindhead?" I asked.

"I thought he said there was a cathedral," Jordan said. "I'm not sure."

"There must be something interesting there," I said.

We passed a great many villages, closed tightly in the Sunday rain. The streets were empty. There were automobile shops and furniture stores, and some deserted-looking nondescript houses. We passed open meadows and groves of trees. Once in a while we went over a bridge.

"The driver isn't pointing out any points of interest," I said.

Mark got out of his seat and came over to us. "What are we going to Hindhead for?" he asked. "What kind of tour is this?"

"I'm not sure," Jordan said.

"Your father thought the man mentioned a cathedral," I said. We all looked at Eric, sitting alone in his seat. He was sucking his thumb and looking out the window. His eyes slithered over to us and then quickly away. He didn't say anything.

We drove and drove, very fast through the rain. The bus was cold and damp.

Bruce got up and came over to us. "I think I'm getting a headache," he said. "Anyway, I'm cold."

"Just be patient," Jordan said. "We'll be there in about an hour and a half."

"An hour and a *half!*" Bruce said.

"See how nice and quiet Eric is," Jordan said. *"He's* not complaining."

We all stared at Eric, who was sucking his thumb and looking out the window.

"He'd better not," Mark said, from across the aisle. Several old people turned to stare at him.

Bruce went back to his seat.

"I just thought of something," I said. "If it takes this long to get there and it's a five-hour trip, that doesn't leave very long to sightsee. I mean it doesn't leave much time for the cathedral."

"You're right," Jordan said.

We drove and drove and drove. Finally it was two and a half hours and we pulled into Hindhead. It was now raining heavily. We drove into the large muddy parking lot of a hotel.

"Hindhead," the driver said. "Leaving again in thirty minutes from here."

A long street stretched in front of us; there were shops on it. Jordan went up to the driver. "Thirty minutes," the driver said, "for tea."

"Tea," Jordan said.

"Yes," the driver said. "But if I was you I wouldn't eat here. There's quite a nice shop down the street. It says 'Scones' in front of it."

We climbed down from the bus and picked our way across the mud to the sidewalk, or pavement. All the old people were trailing toward the Scones shop. We found it without difficulty; it was the only place that was open. It was small and steamy; square wooden tables stood about, covered with oilcloth. We had tea and scones with butter and jelly. Eric ate in silence. Once in a while he smiled at us apologetically.

After we had eaten, we had time for a little stroll. The rain had slowed down to a drizzle. I spied a sundries store with an open door. "Oh, look," I said, excitedly. "We need toilet paper."

We went in, and a man came up to the counter, smiling. "Good afternoon," he said.

"Good afternoon," Jordan said. "We'd like some toilet paper." He pointed to some in a case behind the counter.

The man's smile faded. "Not allowed," he said. "On Sunday."

"You mean…" I said.

"Only medicaments," the man said, "on Sunday." He turned his back to us and we left the shop. We walked across the street and through the muddy parking lot and climbed into the bus. A few old people came running after us, and the bus started back.

Everybody was very jolly on the way back. They called out more often to passing cars and even chatted with each other across the aisle. We drove by more empty villages and deserted houses and groves of trees on the way back; it was impossible to tell whether it was the same route. We went very fast.

"I think we're going faster than we did coming," I observed to Jordan.

"Um," he said. He fell asleep.

Bruce got up and came over to me. "I wish I could sleep like Daddy," he said. "It makes the time go faster."

Eric didn't say anything.

As we approached London, the bus began to stop and deposit passengers on the pavement.

"Bye bye," one called, waving, as she got off. "See you next week. Bye, all."

"Bye bye," the driver said.

We climbed down in Kensington, stiff, cold, tired and full of tea and jam. Jordan made inquiries the next day and found out that all the Green Line Tours were like that. You got on a bus and went some distance and had tea and came back.

32

The Pickwick Club

THE TIME WAS APPROACHING for us to leave for Devon. We made elaborate plans with Mrs. Grail: she was to lock the door of the master bedroom and hide the key in a cookie jar. She was to bolt the front door and leave by the back, hiding the back door key in an accessible spot. We had two back door keys, and we would take one with us. The point of all this plotting was to frustrate Mrs. Stackpole, who we believed had kept a key to the front door in her possession and who kept asking Percy Snell how long we would be gone. We intended to bolt the front door against Mrs. Stackpole, and to lock the bedroom door against her in case, despite our wiles, she was able to penetrate the house.

"Ah, God," Mrs. Grail said. "I know she has a key, and many a time, just think, I'm down in the kitchen and her creeping about upstairs."

Somehow this did not upset me as much as the possibility that what we all heard creeping about upstairs when we were in the kitchen was not only not Mrs. Stackpole, and very probably not even a burglar, but some kind of visitation from another world. We all felt this emanation: to Eric it was simply Hamlet's uncle, but to the rest of us it was nameless. Nobody, including Mrs. Grail, wanted to stay alone in 16 Baldridge Place, even in the daylight hours. Once we left Mark, who wasn't hungry, at home, while we repaired to our Roman spa for dinner. On the way back we encountered him, strolling along the Kensington Road, whistling and trying to look unconcerned. He wasn't wearing his jacket; he had apparently left the house in a hurry. "I couldn't stay in there," he said. "It was odd."

When we got home, he elaborated. "I keep thinking that one night when I'm reading in bed, somebody will knock on my door, and it will open, and a servant will be standing there, holding a candle. Some kind of servant, you know, dressed for the night, with a braid hanging down her back, and holding this candle. She'll just stand there and look at me."

At night we left the sconce in the upper hall burning, and before I went to bed I would stand in the doorway of our bedroom and stare, against my will, at the curving staircase covered with red carpeting, and think that at any moment I would see Mark's servant coming down slowly in the dim light.

None of us cared for 16 Baldridge Place, and it was with happy hearts that we began to pack for five days in Devon, the English Riviera. The night before we were to leave, we sat in the small sitting room wondering if there was any point in turning on the TV, when the telephone rang. The last time it had rung in the evening, it had been a business acquaintance of Jordan's, a lady, who had informed him that she was dying of an asthma attack, and who had croaked, "Come quickly." He had rushed off to Kensington to find that she had croaked the same thing over the phone to ten or twelve other acquaintances, a few of whom had come, bringing doctors. The sound of the telephone ringing did not fill me with pleased anticipation.

"It's Stephanie," he said, muffling the receiver with his hand.

"Who's that?"

"It's that daughter of that friend of my sister's, don't you remember? She's staying at Jane's, she's just arrived. Shall we take her to dinner?"

"Uh," I said.

"How about dinner?" Jordan said into the phone.

"It's after seven now," I said. None of us had wanted dinner because of another five o'clock tea.

"Fine," Jordan said. "We'll pick you up in half an hour." He hung up. "She's leaving for Ireland in the morning. We could hardly not take her to dinner."

"We have to pack," I said, whining.

"You can pack tomorrow. The train doesn't leave until one." I went upstairs, grumbling, and put on a black dress and stockings. I already felt disassociated from London.

"We'll go to the Pickwick Club," Jordan said.

"Ah, God," I said, like Mrs. Grail. "What's that? Another Dickens Room with omelets and minute steaks?"

"It's very nice. Celebrities go there."

We hailed a cab and picked up Stephanie at Jane's place. She was wearing sandals and an upswept hairdo and appeared to be about seventeen years old. She was delighted with herself for coming to Europe alone. I was wearing my dangling earrings and my hair in a bun. Since I was an old habitué of London, I found myself behaving toward Stephanie in a condescending manner. She expressed little curiosity about our situation, and it was shortly apparent that she was laboring under the delusion that we were English.

"My mother knows your relatives," she said to Jordan, "or something. I'm from San Francisco myself, but my mother grew up in a place called Boston. It's in the eastern United States."

"Yes, I know," Jordan said politely.

"Jordan grew up in Boston too," I said.

"Your customs were really quite sticky," Stephanie went on. "I had to wait for ages."

"How do you mean, our customs?" Jordan asked.

"I mean your customs," Stephanie said. "The English customs."

"We're not English," I said, with more emphasis than I would have used two months earlier.

"I loved Copenhagen," Stephanie said. "I'm going to Ireland tomorrow."

"We've been here two months," I said.

"My mother's so worried about me," she said, laughing. "Actually she thinks I'm a baby or something."

"Here we are," Jordan said. "The Pickwick Club."

"Actually, I've never been here before," I told Stephanie. "I don't know what it's like." We went into a bar, and then down some stairs into a cellar-like dining room, empty except for us. We sat in a red velvet banquette against the wall, facing the room.

"It's nice that on her only night in London, we take Stephanie to a place where she can't see anyone," I said.

"It fills up later," Jordan said.

"What a crazy place this is," Stephanie said, referring to England. "Have you noticed the boys' hair?"

"Certainly," I said, in jaded tones. "I've been here two months."

"I can't stand the boys' hair." Stephanie said. 'They look like girls. Do you like it?"

"I like the Beatles," I said.

"Oh, the Beatles," Stephanie said. "They're all right, I guess. For little kids."

"I know some grown women who like them," Jordan remarked.

"Oh, I'm not interested in that sort of thing anymore," she said. "I've outgrown it."

"Indeed," I said.

"I've just been to Copenhagen," she went on. "Have you ever been there?"

We were forced to admit that we had never been to Copenhagen.

"It's awfully interesting," Stephanie said. "They have this park called the Tivoli. And in Paris I saw this cathedral."

"Did you," I said, patting my bun.

Suddenly Stephanie shrieked. "Look at that boy's hair," she said. Some people had come down the stairs, two women and three men.

"Yes," I said. "When one has been in London a while, one hardly notices it."

Stephanie gave a small scream."Look at that hair," she said.

The party was being seated at a long table about five feet from us in the middle of the room. The man at the head of the table began to order, in a pronounced Liverpudlian accent. I stared closely at the boy with the long hair. He floated before my eyes, approaching and receding.

"That's George Harrison," I said with Olympian calm.

"Oh, my God, it's the Beatles," Stephanie said. "Oh, my God, it's John Lennon. And his wife."

It was John Lennon and George Harrison and Mrs. Lennon and Patty Boyd, George Harrison's girlfriend, and Neil Aspinall, the Beatles' road manager. Stephanie sat beside me, moaning.

"Oh, it's the Beatles," she kept saying. "Oh, the Beatles, the Beatles." She rose slightly from her seat. "I'm going over," she said.

"You can't," we said. "Sit down."

"But it's them," she said. "It's them, it's them." She began to rock back and forth.

"Well, you can't go over to them," Jordan said.

Stephanie turned to me. Her eyes were out of focus, and her upswept hairdo had collapsed over one ear. "I have to have their signatures," she said. "Nobody will believe me."

"Calm down," Jordan said.

"You don't understand," she said. "It's them, it's them."

"I'm going to call the kids," Jordan said.

"It's late," I said.

"I don't care. I'm going to call them. This will make up to them for the whole summer."

He checked first with the management, who said the boys could come if they promised to behave quietly, and then he went out to telephone. The phone gave a few of its double bleeps, and Bruce answered. "Hello?" he said.

"Bruce?

"Yes."

"Listen, Bruce," Jordan said tensely. "Listen carefully. I want you to get dressed and give Eric some clothes and tell him to get dressed too. And Mark. Wear something presentable. Get dressed quickly, and go outside and go down to Knightsbridge Road and take a cab, and tell the man you want to go to the Pickwick Club on Great Newport Street off the Charing Cross Road, just above Leicester Square. Remember, the Pickwick Club. Have you got all that?"

There was a long silence. Then Bruce spoke. "Who *is* this?" he said.

"This is your father," Jordan said, exasperated. "Who else could it be?"

"Well, I didn't know," Bruce said."You sounded so funny. You sounded so polite."

"Did you get what I said?"

"No, I didn't," Bruce said. "Here's Mark."

"Yeh?" Mark said, his customary telephone greeting.

"Listen, Mark," Jordan said tensely, "Everybody get dressed, wear something presentable. Go down to the Knightsbridge Road and take a cab, and come to the Pickwick Club on Great Newport Street, off Charing Cross Road, just above Leicester Square. Tell the driver. We're in the restaurant. I'll be waiting for you." He paused. "The Beatles are here. Have you got that?"

"Okay," Mark said. "Goodbye."

Jordan hung up, wondering whether he would ever see them again, and returned to our banquette, where our food had come and Stephanie was still moaning. "They'll be here in five minutes," he said to me.

"I'm going to sit here until they go," I said, referring to the Beatles. "I don't care if I have twelve desserts."

"Oh, please, please," Stephanie said. "Oh, don't you see."

She kept sort of levitating, and we had to hold her down.

After a while Jordan went out to meet the children, and they all came down the stairs. Jordan had told them not to stare, so they came down looking very solemn; their eyes swiveling occasionally to the right. They lined up on the banquette next to me, facing the Beatles, and ordered chocolate cake and milk. John Lennon and George Harrison were wearing black turtlenecks and wheat-colored Levis with wide belts. The women, in long-sleeved shirts, had a great deal of teased blonde hair and black eye makeup.

"This is the unbelievables," Eric whispered to me. "When I get home I'm going to vomit."

"Oh, let me go over there," Stephanie kept saying. "Oh, my only night in London. Oh, oh, oh."

When the Beatles left, we followed them out, and watched them go off in a big black car.

"Oh, why didn't I get their cigarette butts," Mark said. "I wasn't thinking." He went back inside to see if he could remedy the situation.

"When Dad called, Mark screamed and took his sweater off," Bruce said. "I couldn't imagine."

Mark came back disappointed. The ashtrays had already been emptied.

We climbed into a cab which started off well and then smashed into a lamp post. Stephanie, sitting limply at my side with her hair hanging down, refused to notice this.

"I saw Piccadilly at night," Eric said.

"Ah, my God," Stephanie murmured. "My God, my God."

33

Interlude with Chemists

THE NEXT DAY we were to leave for Devon. Bruce awoke with
a large paunchy red eye.

"I'll take him to the doctor," I said to Mrs. Grail, "and then
we'll leave for the station. Mrs. Stackpole will be here at one to
meet our lawyer, Mr. Snell. He'll show her over the house. All
you have to do is let them in, and then remember, you lock the
front door and go out the back—"

"Ah God," Mrs. Grail said, "if you take the little fellow
to the doctor, you'll sit there for hours, it's very hard on such
short notice. Why don't you go to the chemist, he'll give you
something."

"But... buying something in a drug store...?"

"Ah, they have wonderful things in the chemist for that sort
of eye. I bought something from the chemist for that sort of
eye myself once and it worked perfect. If you go to the doctor,
you'll sit all day and you'll miss your train."

I bundled Bruce off down the Brompton Road; Jordan was
to come home in an hour and then we were leaving. It was too
wonderful to be true. The English Riviera. Even Bruce's eye
could not dampen my spirits.

We went into a little chemist's shop.

"And how long has his eye been like this?" the chemist
asked.

I tried to think. "It was sort of getting red a day or two ago," I said.

"A day or two ago!" the chemist said. "We are only given one pair of eyes, Madam, has that occurred to you? Why haven't you taken this child to a physician?"

I took a deep breath. "We are leaving for the country this afternoon," I replied haughtily. "I intend to consult a physician when we arrive. Since we are travelling, I came in here for a stopgap remedy."

I had apparently employed the correct tone; the shopkeeper began to fawn and cringe. "Oh, dear me, Madam, quite right. Oh, please do wait; I shan't be a moment." He returned with a small box. "Just pop this into his eye two or three times a day. It should do the trick. You'll need an eye dropper," he added.

"I shall have to purchase one," I said, still talking funny.

"I'm afraid I'm fresh out."

"We have to get an eye dropper," I said to Bruce, as we left the shop. "I suppose we can get one at Boots." This was a large chemist chain; the nearest one was about five blocks, or fifteen minutes walk, away.

"What a rude man," Bruce said automatically.

"Oh, well," I said

We made our way in a fine drizzle. Ahead of us a young woman, walking fast, was pulling a two-year-old child roughly after her by the hand. The child, trying to keep up, tripped and fell, and the young woman gave her an impatient slap. "Watch out," she said. Before she could haul her tearful offspring on, a very tall majestic woman wearing a turban emerged from the crowd. "You must not pull your child that way, my good woman," the lady said. "The poor little thing cannot keep up.

Don't walk so fast. Poor little thing," she said to the child. She nodded at the mother and went on her way.

The mother stood rooted for a moment, shamefaced, and then moved on, much more slowly. "Come *on,*" she said irritably to the child.

"Did you hear what that man behind me said to the other man?" Bruce asked. "He said, 'We made them,' and the other man said, 'You mean you actually, physically, made them?' and the first man said, 'No, of course not.' What do you suppose he meant?"

"I can't imagine," I said.

"'You mean you actually, physically, made them?'" Bruce said. We went into Boots. A girl in a white coat detached herself from the wall and came over to us. "Yes?" she said. I asked her if she had eye droppers, and she said yes. When she made no move in any direction, I said, "I'd like to buy an eye dropper."

"I'm afraid that's impossible," she said.

"But you have them."

"Oh, yes, we have them, but you see we're cleaning out the cupboard where we keep them, and we've put them in a large box. If you come back next week, I'm sure I can help you then."

"Couldn't you take one out of the box and give it to me?"

"Oh, dear no," she said, smiling. "It's quite a large box. But next week we'll have the cupboard all washed out, I'm sure, and then we'll put everything back and you can have the eye dropper."

"Why didn't they put them in a small box?" Bruce said, as we walked to Harrods.

"Oh, who knows," I responded irritably.

"'You mean you actually, physically, made them?'" Bruce said.

34

The Train

BACK IN BALDRIDGE PLACE we called a cab in a flurry of activity. I told Mrs. Grail once more to remember to bolt the front door and take the back door key, since we were taking the other back door key with us, and to be sure to lock the bedroom door and hide that key in the kitchen. She responded to this, all of which she had heard several times before, and some of which she had suggested herself, with a dazed expression. I knew she was anticipating the meeting with Mrs. Stackpole with dread, if not terror. In her eyes, Mrs. Stackpole had taken on a legendary and menacing aspect, to say the least.

"Have you got it all straight now?" I asked.

"Yes, yes," Mrs. Grail said. "Ah, God."

We scrambled into the cab and went to the station. There we ate ham sandwiches, which to our surprise were very tasty.

"We should have come here for lunch every day," Bruce said. The milk was cold, too.

We boarded the train and after a while it started up and slid smoothly down the track: there was none of the awkward jerking and shaking we had encountered on American trains.

We shared our compartment with a lady from Philadelphia, who had just come from Greece. She was going to stay for a week at a friend's country house in Devon. She traveled a great deal, and she had known England before the war, when, she said, life there was easier. She was an admirably calm, intelligent person.

For miles we passed through a landscape filled with low, dark green hills dotted with grazing sheep. The compartment was comfortable and cozy; the train ran quietly. We were enjoying ourselves. Then we began to feel hungry. Jordan suggested that we have tea in the dining car.

"Why not wait until you get to the hotel?" the lady from Philadelphia asked me, with what I thought was a significant look.

"Oh," I said, "I love to eat on trains. Don't you want to come with us?"

She said she didn't think she would, no.

The others had gone on and I followed them. Outside the dining car, I passed a huge cage thing filled with canvas sacks. If it was the mail, then English people were exclusively occupied in mailing packages of manure to each other. I reeled down the passage to the dining car, where I was overcome by the odor of sour milk, which merged into the other smell. Feeling rather green, I averted my eyes from the kitchen and sat down at a table with Jordan and the boys. I noticed immediately that the waiters were wearing very dirty white coats; in addition, they all seemed to have skin problems, and they were carrying dubious things on their trays.

"What the hell," I said.

"Don't be such a baby," Jordan said automatically.

We had once taken a train from Lyons to Paris; the dining car was not very clean, and neither were the waiters' coats, but the food was excellent, and there was good will in the air, as well as a good smell.

"I'm not going to eat here," I said, getting up.

"Well, I don't know who you're punishing," Jordan said crossly.

"Sit down, Ma," Mark said. Bruce and Eric didn't say anything.

I wended my way back to the compartment, trying not to breathe. The lady from Philadelphia looked at me sympathetically. "I wasn't sure I should say anything," she remarked. I picked up my book, a novel about an Englishman who comes to America to teach at a college and is driven away by the stupidity, narrow-mindedness and ineptitude of everybody on the campus. The book critic for *The Daily Telegraph*, which I read every morning with my breakfast, had praised this novel; he explained that one of the characters, a dishonest hypocritical American English professor, offered a valuable insight into the mind of the American intellectual, and by the same token an insight into what was happening in Vietnam. I had just reached the part where the English protagonist was arrested for taking a walk in the evening, when my family returned.

"So soon?" I asked.

"Ugh," Mark said.

"I could have dealt with it," Jordan remarked. "I could have dealt with it. But that boy, you know, the waiter…"

"The one with the fingernails? Yes."

"Yes, I could have dealt with that, too, but he had this splotch of tomato on his jacket. I don't mean a splotch of ketchup," he went on, "I mean it was a whole tomato, and somehow it had gotten all splotched up against his jacket. You could see the seeds. I lost my appetite."

The lady from Philadelphia nodded at him.

We ate candy bars. I returned to my novel. I wasn't surprised to find the protagonist arrested for taking an evening walk: on various television interview programs, many celebrities returning from the States had earnestly told their audiences that nobody walked in America. One man said he had been arrested for trying to walk a dog.

We began to pass impressively large, rugged cliffs and to catch glimpses of the sea. The lady from Philadelphia left, expressing a heartfelt wish that everything would go smoothly for us. A little while later, the train stopped at Torquay.

35

Arrival at the Castle

WE TOOK A CAB and went down winding hilly road after winding hilly road; there were Victorian houses, some with little front yards and some without. Here and there we saw a palm tree.

"I see you have palm trees here," Jordan said to the cabdriver.

"Oh, yes, it's quite warm here all winter," the driver said.

"What sort of hotel is the Castle?" Jordan asked.

"Oh, it's a five star hotel. Oh, it's very elegant. Cost a fortune to put up."

At a considerable distance from the railway station, we drove through tall gates surrounded by greenery and stopped at a portico before the entrance to the hotel, which was constructed of stone. The lobby was carpeted in red with enormous yellow and green flowers, and filled with fat, nineteen-thirtyish "modernistic" furniture.

Upstairs we were escorted to a three-room suite: large and light and spotlessly clean, painted white, with white furniture. Our room had a balcony looking out on to the Castle grounds: these were undulating and heavily planted with evergreen trees, dense and green to the point of blackness. I was reminded forcibly of *The Magic Mountain*. I could see myself lying on a chaise on the balcony, wrapped in a blanket, staring at the thick silent forest.

Mark said it was cool.

"I wonder why everything is white," Jordan said. "It looks like a hospital. You do like it, don't you?" he asked me, anxiously.

"It's marvelous," I said sincerely. "It's awfully nice."

It was dinner time, so we went downstairs. The dining room was enormous, with large windows and off-white paneled walls. Through the windows you could see the omnipresent, brooding grounds; the trees were always still.

On the table was a plate of toast, cold and curled, the only form of bread available at the Castle Hotel. We had a cheerful young uniformed waiter. He brought us big soup plates, each with half an inch of clear soup nestled in the bottom.

"Meals must be included," Jordan said.

After the soup was taken away, we were brought a plate of fish fillet with red sauce. Then came a small slice of meat, faintly lamby, on a large plate. In addition, the waiter passed around two kinds of potatoes and some varieties of bean. At this point some very old musicians filed in, took their places on a low platform directly behind us, and broke into an awful cacophony that raised all the small hairs on the back of my neck. It appeared to be a tune from *Mary Poppins,* played in march tempo.

"What's that?" we asked the waiter.

"Harry Evans and the Orchestra," he replied. He took away our plates. For dessert we were offered a "choice of cold sweets from the trolley." They were rainbow-colored and trembled slightly. "We also have Castle Pudding with jam sauce," the waiter said.

The other diners were middle-aged, and looked strangely out of date: the women had marcelled hair and bosomy print dresses; the men's suits had wide shoulders and wide pleated pants, or trousers. The familiar *Time Machine* sensation crept over me.

"Sometimes in London," I said, "I felt as though I had gone back eighty years. It was weird. But here… it could be nineteen thirty-five. Don't you think so?"

"I wish you wouldn't overstate things," Jordan said. "It could easily be nineteen thirty-nine."

Mark said it was wild.

All eyes followed us as we left the dining room. I felt rather flashy in my Mary Quant dress with the outrageous hemline. We went upstairs and watched television, on a set that we had ordered, for an hour. It was even more horrible than London television: the clergyman who read the evening sermon looked as though he were melting. I put the drops in Bruce's eye and tucked the children in. Then Jordan and I took a cab to the Imperial Hotel: the cabdriver told us it was the best hotel in Torquay.

"Maybe it's more modern than the Castle?" Jordan asked hopefully.

"Oh, the old Castle's gone down," the driver said. "Once it was five star. Now I think it's only three. But the Imperial's very nice. Royalty stay there."

The Imperial had a swimming pool and a beach, and no furniture in the lobby. The people wandering about were slender and none of them had finger waves.

"We're full up," the girl said. "Sorry." Back we went to the Castle and so to bed.

36

Life at the Castle

THE NEXT MORNING we were shown to the same table, which had obviously been assigned to us, with the same tablecloth in the condition in which we had left it the night before. The napkins were the same too, but they had been neatly folded and placed in rings. I was surprised that Eric's napkin had been preserved, but in Rome you know. Jordan and Eric had hot cereal for breakfast and we all had eggs. The toast was cold but not curled. I noticed that an unprepossessing woman at the next table was staring at me fixedly.

"That woman's staring at me," I said to Jordan.

"Ignore her," he advised, but it was difficult because I was facing her. She sat and stared; she even stared while she ate.

After breakfast we walked out into the grounds. They were very expansive, and encompassed a golf course. If you went far enough, walked over a little bridge and down a flight of stone steps, you could reach a small harbor just behind the hotel. A boardwalk overlooked the rocky beach with its small stretch of gritty sand. While the children climbed gingerly over the rocks, Jordan and I sat in rented chairs, enveloped by pale watery sunshine. Nobody was swimming; apart from the fact that we could see sharp stones littering the shallow bottom, it was too cold to swim. We were glad that we were all wearing sweaters.

There were a great many young people there. None of them wore shorts: some of the girls were in slacks, but most of them were wearing summer dresses. They carefully folded their skirts back as they sat sunning their white legs. Jordan and I began to talk about the train. I thought we had lowered our voices, until I turned my head and realized that my neighbor had been hanging on our every word.

"She says the train smells of sour milk," she announced to her companions. "The train's lovely, isn't it?"

I felt I had done my bit for international relations that morning. The sky clouded over and drops began to fall. We called the children and went back to the hotel for lunch. Once more we were served cold curled toast, clear soup, a fish course, a meat course, two kinds of potatoes, and cabbage. The sweets glowed and trembled on the trolley. "Have a Glass of Wine with your Meals," the menu suggested.

After lunch the children went to swim in the indoor pool, and Jordan and I took a bus into Torquay; we sat on the open top in the light rain. Torquay was filled with shops; we browsed for a while in the paperback section of a large bookstore. Most of the crowd in the streets looked like extras for one of those post-war British films about working-class life. The men wore cloth caps and the women wore curlers. There were posters everywhere announcing a beauty contest in Babbacomb.

We returned to the hotel, helped the children clean up after their afternoon of swimming in the dank and chilly pool room, and descended once again for dinner. This time the soup was Creamed Asparagus, but the bowl was just as big and the portion just as small as the Clear Soups. There was fish in a white sauce, and Grenadin of Veal, tasting faintly lamby. We had the two kinds of potato, and some cauliflower.

The menu had a choice of three entrees on it.

"What's forcemeat and chipolata?" Mark asked.

"Turkey, I think," Jordan said, "and sausage."

"I couldn't eat anything called forcemeat," Mark said.

The woman at the next table was still staring at me. She picked her tooth with her fingernail, wiped the nail ostentatiously on her napkin, and went on staring.

"She's still staring at me," I complained, "and what's more I think she's revolting."

"Change places with Mark," Jordan said. So I sat in Mark's place with my back to the revolting starer.

"She's saying something to her husband and pointing at us," Mark announced.

"Rhubarb and apple tart for dessert," the waiter said, "or Windsor jellies, of course."

Jordan asked if coffee could be served with dessert.

"Coffee is served in the lounge, sir," the waiter said, "after dinner."

"But we'd like it with dessert."

"I'll see what can be arranged," the waiter said.

Nothing could be arranged, because dessert was served without coffee. We went into the lounge, sat in the fat chairs and watched the rain streaking the tall windows. There were several fireplaces in the lounge, but they were cold and empty. An icy wind whistled about our ears. The children went off to explore, and came back excited.

"Hey, there are slot machines back there," Bruce said. "Can I have a shilling?"

We gave them money, and they went away. There were slot machines in "arcades" all over Torquay. In a little while Mark came rushing in to announce that he had won the jackpot.

We trailed after him to the sun porch. In addition to dusty wicker furniture, it housed a collection of slot machines made in Chicago, and one of those machines with a claw that fishes out plastic combs and thimbles, and avoids the cameras and binoculars that enticed you in the first place. There were a lot of children and adults in the porch; no one reached out the hand of friendship to the traveler. Our children had always made friends in the many hotels we had stayed at in America. Here they were regarded with a decidedly fishy eye. I thought about the reception an English family would have at an American resort. Maud Tweak had touched on this topic with me at our party.

"We are not quick to make friends," she said, "but when we do make friends, I'm afraid our friendships last longer than yours do."

After the money was gone, we went upstairs and I put the drops in Bruce's eye, which was much improved. Eric was complaining about a gumboil. We watched some clergymen on television and then turned in.

The next morning, after our hot cereal and eggs, we repaired once again to the beach; this time Jordan and the boys went out in a motor boat until the rain drove them to shore again. For lunch we ate our soup, our toast, our fish, a very small lamb chop tasting faintly lamby, boiled potatoes, creamed potatoes and buttered runner beans. Eric refused everything and looked out the window at the steady rain on the dark trees.

"Are you sick?" I asked.

"I hate this food," he said. "My gumboil hurts."

I noticed that he had dark smudges under his eyes and his face was the size and color of a slice of lemon. "He's starving,"

I said to Jordan, alarmed. "He must have a gumboil because of vitamin deficiency."

"Don't you want your potatoes?" Jordan asked Eric.

"No," Eric said, and sighed.

After lunch we all went into Torquay on the bus. The town was packed; it was difficult to make our way down the street. We bought ice cream and passed a movie: *Help*.

"We'll see that tomorrow," Jordan said.

We took a taxi back to the hotel and hung around till dinner. Eric ate a little, helping himself to boiled potatoes from the waiter's serving dish.

"Say 'thank you,'" Jordan said to Eric.

"Oh, it's all right," the waiter said. "He hasn't been in England long enough to learn 'please' and 'thank you'." He went off with his dish.

"Did you hear that?" I asked, seething.

"He didn't mean it that way," Mark said.

"'What do you mean? What other way could he mean it?'"

"Oh, Ma," Mark said.

"Did you hear that?" I asked Bruce.

"No, I didn't catch it," Bruce said.

"Eat up," Jordan said. "It isn't every day you have braised Wilshire ham with noodles."

"No, thank God," I said.

"That woman is glaring at us," Mark observed.

Harry Evans and the Orchestra were in fine fettle.

"That noise is driving me crazy," Jordan said.

We took our coffee in the lounge and the children went off to play table tennis. I sat and read. After a while the boys went back to the wicker room to try and win the jackpot again, and then we went up to bed.

The next morning we had two hours on the boardwalk before the rain started, and then we went into town to see *Help*, starring the Beatles. We walked in line, realized we would have to miss lunch, and bought candy bars instead. *Help* was on a double bill with a terrible American picture. We ate a lot of candy bars and watched *Help*; we found it less appealing than *A Hard Day's Night*. We were in fact bewildered by it. That may have been due to our situation at the time, because when we saw it again months later, we enjoyed it. We returned to the hotel for tea: bread and butter and mashed sardines. After that the children gambled until dinner.

The next day was our last in Devon. There were specialties for sale in Torquay, like Devonshire cream and apple cider, but they were not available in the hotel, and the shops were literally too crowded to enter. "Where do all the people come from?" we asked the waiter at lunch, as he removed our soup plates and before he brought the fish course.

"The factories close in the Midlands in August," he said. "Most of the people come down here for their holiday."

I had read in a pamphlet that the English Riviera had come into being as a result of the Napoleonic wars. Nobody could go to the Continent, so they came to Devon and Cornwall instead. I could certainly sympathize with them: the same thing had happened to us. We hadn't been able to get to the Continent either.

Lunch ended, and the sun was still shining. This was unprecedented, so we decided to do some sightseeing. Not far away was a little village called Cockington Forge; it was supposed to be preserved in an ancient state. We all piled into a taxi and off we went.

Cockington Forge consisted mainly of souvenir shops. We strolled along a path leading through a grassy park, dotted here and there with large signs saying "Toilets." There was an old church on a hill: it was very old, dating from Norman times. We read all about it, and examined the restorations; they looked very convincing to us. There was a café near the church, but we didn't go in. We had just had lunch, and, too, something about the look of it reminded us of the café in London where you couldn't sit at the table unless you ordered a meal, even if you were the only one in a large party who wasn't hungry, and where all the crockery and silver was chipped and/or greasy.

We walked back down the hill to the shops to see what we could buy. There were a lot of brass ashtrays and little bells, and china ducks and cuckoo clocks. We called a cab and went outside to sit in the sun and wait for it. It was actually warm, although rather damp and stuffy. Eventually the cab came and took us back to Torquay.

The boys went outside for a while. When it started to rain, they came back in; we gave them each half a crown and they went off to gamble. Then we got dressed for our final dinner at the Castle Hotel. I put on my dangly earrings and my Mary Quant dress and we went downstairs. In the hall near the elevator, or lift, was a smallish room for the maids. An overpowering smell of fish emanated from it, mixed with something like cocoa. I held my breath and hurried down the stairs; the lift never seemed to be in operation.

For dinner we had Creamed Vegetable Soup, which tasted like Creamed Asparagus Soup. Then we had Grilled Lamb Chop, one small chop apiece. It tasted faintly lamby.

Eric ate a boiled potato; his face looked more like a slice of lemon than ever. The vegetable was buttered Brussels sprouts.

"I'll be glad to get back to London again," Jordan said, "to get something to eat, and I never thought I'd say *that*."

Harry Evans and the Orchestra were playing something with violins in it. A very fat blonde lady with an upswept hairdo and a flowered décolletage kept time with her fork against a water glass.

"I don't believe this place," Mark said. "I don't, I can't."

"Tapioca Milk Pudding," the waiter said, "Normandy Pudding, or of course the cold sweets from the trolley." He gestured toward them, and they winked at us, shimmering in five colors.

"Does anyone ever complain about Harry Evans and the Orchestra?" Jordan asked him, emboldened by the approach of our departure.

"Oh," the waiter replied, "he's been here so long I expect everyone has forgotten why he ever started in the first place. Nobody ever thinks about him one way or the other."

We took the puddings. "That woman is still staring at us," Mark said. "Now she's saying something to her husband. Wait a minute, she's choking."

A ragged noise of coughing rose in the air behind my back.

"I think she's choking to death," Mark reported. "He's getting up. He's pounding her on the back. She looks like a hippopotamus with a bird caught in its throat."

"That's hardly kind," I said, because I thought I should.

"She's all right now," Mark said, in a disappointed voice.

"This pudding is full of lumps," Bruce said.

We decided to pack it in, and rose as a family. As I passed the Staring Woman, she turned to her husband and said loudly, "Funny looking creature, isn't she?"

While we sipped our coffee in the lounge, Mark fumed and fretted. "Did you hear it?" he kept saying. "Did you hear what she said?"

"Actually," Bruce said to me, "she's funnier looking than you are."

We went into the large and echoey table tennis room and played table tennis. After a while footsteps pounded outside the door and two fat little girls whom we had seen in the wicker room, dashed in. "Where's Bruce?" they screamed. We were all, including Bruce, surprised that they knew his name.

"The jackpot's been won!" one of the little girls announced, and the other called loudly, "British luck wins again!" They paused for a moment of triumph and darted out again.

"None of them said a word to me when *I* won," Mark said. I pointed out that he wasn't British.

* * *

We all felt lighthearted while we waited in the station for the train to carry us back to London, even though Mrs. Stackpole's gloomy little house awaited us. It was still a relief to get away from the cold curled toast and faint lamb, to say nothing of the xenophobia in close quarters. Eric, although looking far from well, donned his French Harlequin red-framed sunglasses, his corduroy Beatles cap, and, holding an unlighted cigarette that he had mooched from Jordan, climbed up onto a varnished station bench in his sneakers, and put his hand inside his coat.

"My name is Nelson," he said. "I got a gumboil."

A lady in a flowered hat, sitting on another bench some distance from us, began to twitch with annoyance. She turned to a young man sitting next to her, and discussed us audibly.

"My name is Nelson," Eric said in clipped tones. "My gumboil hurts."

"Don't stand on the furniture, dear," the woman called. She twitched again, and her glassy-eyed, chinless companion nodded at her in dim approval.

Eric took a drag of his unlighted cigarette and climbed down from the bench.

37

Back Again

AND SO WE TOOK OUR LEAVE of rainy Devon, famous for cream and cider, neither of which was served in the hotel, and returned to London on a bleak cold Sunday afternoon in August. Awaiting us was a letter from Percy Snell.

"Oh, goody," I said. "It's probably about his going over the house with Mrs. Stackpole. I bet she never expected a lawyer to meet her."

"It's the only way to handle people like her," Jordan said, and read the letter.

"… accompanied Mrs. Stackpole about the house as you requested. We discovered a great deal of damage had been done as a result of a tap being carelessly left running. Do you know anything about this?

"In addition, Mrs. Stackpole was terribly upset because the front door had not been locked. As she pointed out to me, there have been several robberies in the neighborhood recently, and she is understandably alarmed. I have told her that I would tell you this, since neither of us could understand why the front door had been left in this condition."

"What kind of letter is this from a lawyer?" I asked. "Whose lawyer is he anyway?"

"I told that half-wit about the tub," Jordan said irritably.

"I know he knew about it," I said, "because I talked to him about Mr. MacAllister harassing me. He laughed."

"He's an idiot," Jordan said.

I was also annoyed that Mrs. Grail had apparently charged out in a panic, not locking our bedroom door, not bolting the front door, and not taking the basement key.

"Ah, I thought I heard her in the house," she said. "Her creeping about and me downstairs. I couldn't stick it, so I left."

We could hardly blame her for feeling like that. No one wanted to stay in that house alone. Or even in part of the house alone.

"Of course she complained to Mr. Snell about the door not being properly locked," I said crossly.

"Ah, Mr. Snell," Mrs. Grail cried. "Ah, the look of him. A great fat thing with a moon face, and them dead blue eyes."

"I know the type," I said, thinking of Mr. MacAllister.

"Ah, God," Mrs. Grail said, "thick as thieves, the two of them. 'You can go home, Mrs. Grail,' he says to me, and I says, 'No, the lady told me to stay until two and I'm staying.'"

"He got on well with Mrs. Stackpole, I guess," I said.

"Got on?" Mrs. Grail said. "Thick as thieves, the two of them. Well, you're a foreigner, aren't you, and they both English? Look out for them, they'll do you every time. And another woman was here. Yes, she brought in another woman, as a witness, I suppose. A great fat thing came running, in an apron."

"He didn't mention that," I said.

"No, he wouldn't tell you that, would he? And them smiling and nodding, cozy as could be, and 'Mrs. Grail, you can go now.' It's the English; they'll do you every time."

The phone rang. "Is this the Stackpole residence?" a voice inquired. "We are calling to make an appointment for the carpet cleaning."

"What carpet cleaning?"

"Is this the tenant? Mrs. Stackpole called us on Friday and told us to make arrangements with you for the carpet cleaning. She said you would see to it."

"She was wrong," I said grimly, and hung up.

"Ah, God," Mrs. Grail said softly.

It was clear that Eric needed a doctor. I made an appointment with Mrs. Bilkington's Dr Killman. We took a cab in the rain to a street very near the bus depot, the scene of another one of our fiascos, and the cab double-parked across from the doctor's office building. I got out to pay the driver, saying "Don't move," to Eric, who immediately darted into the middle of the road. A small car screeched to a halt a foot away from him; the driver sat paralyzed behind the wheel. Eric, who had executed a sort of tribal dance when he saw the car bearing down on him, appeared rather subdued. I was shaking too much to yell at him as we wended our way into the office.

"Eric Miller, for his appointment," I announced to the receptionist. She nodded and made a note. I sank onto a sofa. "I feel quite weak," I said. "I just had an awful experience."

"I know," the receptionist said with a smile. She gestured toward the window. "I saw it."

I had in fact glimpsed several heads protruding from an upstairs window as I had trembled my way toward Eric. She resumed her work, and in a little while the doctor admitted us. He was a bluff but pleasant sort who seemed to know his business.

"Are you going to give me a throat culture?" Eric asked.

"No," Dr. Killman said. "I only give throat cultures when they're necessary. I'm an English doctor, not an American one." It developed that Eric had an infection and needed an antibiotic. I had a cold, so the doctor prescribed an antihistamine for me that could be filled at Harrods, but not at Boots. It seemed that pharmacies had their own lists and used their own judgment.

While Eric recovered, the boys stayed in and played checkers. I walked to Harrods in the rain and bought other games. Our desire to see the sun became an obsession; it was clear that Eric and Bruce and I could never last in London until the first week of September. It was finally decided that the three of us would leave in eight days, on the twenty-first of August. Mrs. Grail had announced her husband's vacation or holiday; it was only for four days. They were going to Ireland, but she would be back Monday.

"But give me your address in America," she said. "For a Christmas card."

"But I'll see you when you get back," I said.

"Just give me your address," she said ominously.

She did not return on the following Monday, and we never heard from her again. I couldn't find the dustpan, and things fell into disrepair. I gave up all pretense of trying to shop and cook; every night we went for dinner to Peter Evans where the portions were small but good. There was the sense of an ending.

During all this, Basil Goldbrick actually bought into the business. About time too: I received an agitated phone call from Bill Dworkin, whom the Pressclips employees referred to as Mr. Dorking. "Do you know where Jordan is?" Bill asked, in a throaty whisper.

"Why, no. Don't you?"

"He and Basil Goldbrick went to the bank," Bill said, "to get the money for the payroll. Basil has to sign something or the bank won't give us any more money. It's almost four, and... and..." he laughed nervously. "I'm all alone here now, and they're beginning to look at me kind of funny. I think they're all moving toward me. It's payday."

"My God," I said reassuringly. "I hope for your sake Jordan comes back soon."

"Some of these ladies are rather peculiar," Bill whispered. "I wish he'd hurry."

It turned out that it was too late to get the money from the bank, but Basil Goldbrick, whose source of income was obscure and who wore colorless nail polish, happened to have the amount of the payroll in his pocket. Since, as I have said, English workers wouldn't take checks because they were only pieces of paper and didn't jingle, it was a lucky thing for Bill, at least, that Basil happened to turn up loaded.

In any case, the business was saved, Mrs. Grail was gone, and Eric and Bruce and I had exhausted most possibilities.

It was time to think of moseying on.

38

Crockford's

AS A SORT OF FAREWELL GESTURE, Basil and Daisy Goldbrick invited us to dinner at Crockford's, the private gambling club where Cynthia had hoped to glimpse titled people. The club, unlighted on the outside, was in a large old white house on a dead end street. Daisy was a vision of loveliness in white wool, and Basil was wearing his nail polish, his cufflinks, his moustache and his floppy collar. We were introduced to Mr. Phenix, a small, very dark man who looked like a Turkish double agent from an Eric Ambler novel, and to Daisy's niece and nephew from Liverpool who greeted us in rich Yorkshire accents. Daisy herself spoke carefully, with great precision.

"Mr. Phenix, you know," she said to me, "is a descendant of the Duke of Phoenix, a Spanish aristocrat."

"Yes, that's quite right," Basil said. We all looked at Mr. Phenix, who smiled enigmatically.

Basil asked me what I would like for a first course. I said I didn't know.

"What would you have if you were in America?" Mr. Phenix asked me.

"I'd have a shrimp cocktail," I said.

"Well, you can have that here," Mr. Phenix said, nodding briskly to the waiter, who wrote it down at once. When they came, they were not of course American shrimp, but rubbery little English prawns. I told Mr. Phenix they were delicious.

"You don't get quite the portions here that you do in America," Basil observed. "I know you won't mind my saying this," he went on, "but when Daisy and I were in Chicago, we used to go to the beach, and I must say we were appalled at the appearance of the people. They were all so hideously fat."

"My goodness, yes," Daisy said. "One noticed that they were all so dreadfully fat."

"I expect that's because they eat too much," the niece remarked.

"Oh, the portions in the restaurants," Basil said. "Oh, they're over-facing."

"I don't think of Jordan as a typical American," the niece observed.

"Oh, heavens," Daisy responded. "Oh, heavens, no. Jordan? Not typical at all."

"There are so many things about the United States we don't understand," the niece said, in lilting Liverpool. "Bigotry, for one thing. We don't understand bigotry at all here. It frightens me."

I looked at the niece for a long moment, and she looked back at me, batting her big vacant blue eyes in fear. "We're frightened of bigotry," she said, "because we don't understand it."

"One is always frightened of what one doesn't understand, Giselle," Daisy said graciously.

"I certainly agree," Mr. Phenix said. "One is, isn't one?"

"I've been so anxious to speak with you, Anita," Daisy said. "I said to Basil just the other day that I was so anxious to speak with you."

I was eating with some relish, because the food did not taste English. It was heavy with wild rice and full of cream sauce, but it tasted familiar, like the food served on airplanes.

"I was in Chicago for some months at one time," Daisy said. She sounded as though she was in an elocution class, reading from a paper entitled "My Summer Vacation." "I was feeling most downhearted at the time, and I thought, well, I will go away. I will go somewhere far away. So I went to Chicago, because I had a friend there in a place called Des Plaines. She was an old friend of mine, from quite a nice English family, who had moved to America, so I assumed that Des Plaines would be quite pleasant." She paused to take a drink of water. "However," she resumed, "I found to my sorrow that such was not the case."

"Not the case?" Mr. Phenix asked.

"No," Daisy replied, "not at all the case." She cleared her throat. "I entered the plane, feeling most downhearted. I was wearing a very attractive hat, however. The hat was tall, you see, with taffeta stripes. I sat next to a most unattractive woman, heavy, you know, and far from young. She proceeded to tell me that her fiancé—her fiancé, mind you was meeting her in Chicago." She paused and smiled. "Here was this woman... old, unattractive, badly dressed... with a fiancé, and here was *I*... quite alone."

She paused again, to let the shock seep through us.

"Gracious," I said, through the cream sauce.

Daisy smiled again. "I thought, 'My, I must indeed be unattractive, if I... have no one.' I sat there, feeling most down. And then the co-pilot came to fetch me. The pilot had sent him, to invite me to the cabin, because of my hat!" She laughed merrily, showing even white teeth. "Oh, what a time we had," she said, "in the pilot's cabin."

I missed several chapters of her story because of chewing a hard roll, which caused a sort of roaring in my ears. "And imagine my surprise," she was saying, "when my dear friend in Des Plaines seemed quite indifferent on the phone!"

"How rude of her," Mr. Phenix commented. "Is she an American?"

Even I remembered that the dear friend in Des Plaines was English.

"No, my dear," Daisy said. "But how changed! I went to stay with her. She was married to an Italian, an Italian truck driver...."

"An Italian?" Jordan said.

"Well, an American of Italian descent. He was a truck driver." Daisy closed her eyes. "It's painful to me," she whispered, "even now."

"What did he do?" I asked, all agog. I visualized the Italian chasing Daisy around Des Plaines.

"I can't... even now..." she drew a deep breath and looked at us. "You can imagine my feelings," she said, in a low voice, "when I discovered that this man... that he had never heard of Dickens."

"Fancy that," Mr. Phenix said.

"*You* can understand," Daisy said to me. "My dear friend had married this man... he had never heard of..."

After dinner, we went upstairs and watched a lot of well-dressed people gamble. Daisy's nephew, who was a physical education teacher, explained to us about chemin-de-fer. I stood next to an American lady who didn't seem typical, and she and I chatted.

"You spoke to Daisy at the table," Basil said to me, twitching his moustache. "Marvelous raconteur, isn't she?"

"Oh, oh," I said.

"Tell them the story about the dog, Daisy," Basil said.

"Oh, I am feeling quite tired, Basil," Daisy said, pressing the back of her hand against her fluffy bangs. Or fringe.

We put the Liverpool couple into a taxi and got into Basil's car. After we were settled in, Daisy told us the story about the dog. It seemed she had this poodle, which was hardly a surprise, and it climbed on Basil's bed, and he kept shouting at it to get out of his room and of course the landlady, who lived upstairs, thought he was shouting at *Daisy*."

"Oh, a marvelous story," Basil said, wiping his eyes. He gave me a healthy nudge.

"Did you ever hear anyone tell stories the way Daisy does?" he asked.

"No, I never did," I said truthfully.

"I must explain that our young couple came down unexpectedly," Daisy said, turning her head gracefully on her swanlike neck. "I really am quite exhausted, but one must cope with everyone. Oh, they're quite sweet, really."

That took care of the physical education teacher and his frightened wife.

"Tell them the story about the painting," Basil said. "You know Daisy paints," he informed us.

"I see she does," I replied, and received a poke from Jordan, but it didn't matter because they weren't listening to me anyway.

39

Deathbed Wish

ON AUGUST 21ST, I flew home with Eric and Bruce, leaving Jordan and Mark to join us in time for Mark to start school. Jordan had to return to London to oversee the transfer of management of Pressclips U.K. from himself and Bill Dworkin to Basil Goldbrick's people. Jordan took a small flat at 45 Ennismore Gardens in Kensington, and there he received notice from our Percy Snell, of the large prestigious firm of Bartram & Goldfleet, that one F.E.H. Mantrap of Fulger & Gammon had contacted him on behalf of Mrs. Stackpole with the following claims:

Electricians Bill £3.11.6

Removal of marks and other stains
from carpets 4. 10. 0

Breakages: 1 bowl, 1 bulb and one cup . . . . 1. 0. 0.

Laundry bill. . . . . 3. 0. 1.

Removal of bottle marks from Queen Anne
table and damage thereto . . . . .7. 10. 0.

We settled these mysterious claims—there was no Queen Anne table in the house; we hadn't broken anything; the carpet stains had been there when we arrived; any more recent stains had resulted from the defective drain flood ignored by Mr. MacAllister, and we had paid all bills engendered by us—for an amount roughly equivalent to twelve dollars. Mrs. Stackpole and Mr. Mantrap thus passed out of our lives forever.

Percy Snell, on the other hand, had not passed out of our lives, because Jordan was entangled with Basil Goldbrick and the English press clipping bureau. All sorts of papers had to be drawn up and signed, and it was July of 1966 before Jordan could come home more or less for good. Basil hired one Gilbert Cradge to run the bureau, and began to charge various personal expenses to it; this of course might eat up any possible profits, but Jordan didn't complain because he was deeply grateful to Basil for having taken over total responsibility. Basil and Gilbert sent the occasional cheery note, and the business seemed to be running as well as could be expected. If it showed a profit, Jordan was entitled to a return on his investment.

In April of 1969, Jordan and I went back to London; this time we were able to stay at Dolphin Square, in a dry, warm, comfortable apartment. Dolphin Square is a block of permanent and transient flats erected on the Embankment before World War II. We arrived after the usual sleepless jet-lagged night, and Jordan rushed off in the usual cold rainstorm to the Pressclips office to see his old pals and check on how things were going.

To his horror, he found the office entryway blocked by various husky persons carrying Pressclips furniture out to a large moving van, or lorry, in the street. One of the clipping employees happened to be standing there. "Oh, hello, Mr. Miller," she said warmly, "How've you been?"

"What," Jordan said, "Where...?"

"Oh, we're moving to the Isle of Wight," she said, "Nice to see you again."

Jordan returned home with a raging head cold, and spent several days of our holiday hanging over the electric fire with a towel over his head. From that moment, his feelings toward Basil Goldbrick were never the same—especially since Basil was less than responsive to phone calls and letters. Jordan wanted Arthur Anderson, an independent accounting firm, to audit the Pressclips books, but made no headway with this because Basil's accountants, Blackleg & Crum, had perpetual difficulty coming up with the figures. Percy Snell, in response to Jordan's increasingly frantic appeals, explained that there really wasn't anything anyone could do. For the better part of three years, Jordan fired off letters to Percy, who in turn communicated with Blackleg & Crum. At the end of that time, word reached us that Basil Goldbrick had shaken off this mortal coil. He was no more.

After a decent interval, Jordan returned to the fray. Gilbert Cradge was apparently running the company for Daisy Goldbrick, now that Basil had left the scene. Jordan told Percy Snell that he had to have an accountant.

"This is ridiculous," Jordan said. "I have to have access to the books."

"Well, you see," Percy said, "Gilbert Cradge and Blackleg & Crum have all told me that on his deathbed, Basil's last words were, 'Don't pay Jordan.' This makes it very difficult."

Frustrated, Jordan decided to fire Percy Snell. Burton Thigpen, of the large prestigious firm of Conquest & Weed, came highly recommended; so we went up to his elegant offices in the Aldwych to talk to him. Burton was sympathetic, and the offices seemed pleasantly laid back—when I went to use the attractive ladies room, I shared the sinks with a woman who was washing out a head of lettuce—so Jordan hired Burton. It took longer than we realized for Jordan to explain everything to him, and when we emerged into the Aldwych we discovered that our rented car had been towed away.

We took a cab to the police car pound in the East End. There the police were more than sympathetic. They asked how long we had been in England. We told them we'd been there almost three weeks.

"No, no," they said. "You've been here a week."

"No, we haven't," Jordan said. "We've been here almost three weeks. We came—let me see—"

"No, no," they kept saying. "You haven't been here that long." They were looking at us significantly. We didn't get it. Finally one of them said, "Since you've only been here a week, you aren't going to be charged for the towing." Then we got it.

This was a tourist-friendly British gesture, and the policemen and women couldn't have been nicer. The atmosphere was certainly benign, as it had not been in our Knightsbridge days several years earlier. We were happy to detect a thaw in the attitude toward Americans. Of course we were no longer in touch with Maud Tweak. Despite this welcome improvement in the general atmosphere, we were forced after several months to face the fact that Burton Thigpen not only looked like Percy Snell—and therefore of course like Mr. MacAllister—but shared Percy's ingrained inability to get anything done. Blackleg & Crum kept presenting innumerable reasons why they couldn't give Jordan access to the Pressclips figures.

We returned to London and took Gilbert Cradge, a very thin friendly person in his thirties, to dinner. Gilbert confided to us that Basil had absolutely drained the company and there was no money left at all. His feelings toward Basil lacked warmth.

"He wasn't any help," Gilbert said. "He used to sit and doze in his office. I often thought," he remarked softly, leaning toward us over his fish plate, "I often thought how simple it would be just to take a cushion from his sofa and hold it over his face while he was sleeping there."

We decided on the basis of this comment that we did not want to have anything more to do with Gilbert Cradge, and we were sorry that we had taken him to dinner. When we got back to Dolphin Square that night, we toyed with the idea of calling Daisy Goldbrick and warning her against falling asleep in Gilbert's presence, but we decided that she would probably not accept advice from us.

We expressed frustration to an English acquaintance, who told us to forget about Burton Thigpen and Conquest & Weed.

"What you need is a different type of lawyer," she said. "You need a young lawyer from a small firm, somebody fresh who needs the business, who knows how to work."

This sounded sensible to us. She gave us the name of Norman Ziman. So Jordan fired Burton and hired Norman, who was different physically and in every other way from Mr. MacAllister, Percy Snell and Burton Thigpen.

Norman ran into the usual difficulties with Blackleg & Crum, but he had a suggestion for Jordan. "You know," he said, "as a shareholder in this company, you can actually bankrupt it if you choose. Of course you'd lose your investment. But as a last resort, perhaps we can threaten them with this."

We didn't have to think about this very long. It looked as though our investment was going to be lost anyway. We didn't think we had much to lose. So Norman told Blackleg & Crum that Jordan was going to bankrupt the company if he didn't get paid.

At first, they thought this was amusing. "You'll lose all your money," Harvey Blackleg said to Jordan, with a chuckle. When Jordan said he was too angry to care, Harvey clearly didn't believe him. But as Norman put the bankruptcy procedure into operation, they began to realize that this was no laughing matter. After weeks and weeks of bluster and protest, and on the very eve of the winding up of the company—with literally hours to go—they capitulated, produced the books, agreed to pay Jordan off, and did actually pay him, in quarterly installments.

Thus ended our English press clipping venture. But we could not seem to break off our connection with England. Somehow we became book publishers—often called the accidental profession—and since we could not overcome our predilection for the English novel and English books in general, our publishing house inevitably bore an Anglophile stamp. Our publishing experiences with the English were certainly more positive than our clipping episodes had been. For one thing, we didn't meet anyone like Maud Tweak in publishing, and we rented no houses in Knightsbridge. This is not to say that bizarre adventures did not befall us in our new incarnation—but that is another story.